What People Are Saying About Jo Naughton and
30-Day Detox for Your Soul

This book is a gift from God to change your life. Jo has given us a manual to mend the broken heart and to give a rudderless ship hope and new direction. Just as we detox the body to rid ourselves of poisons, we must detox our hearts and minds by God's Spirit so that we can accomplish our mission on the earth. Jo has unique insight and real wisdom and is qualified from the vantage point of having walked this out in her own life. As you do this *30-Day Detox*, allow the Holy Spirit to lead you into a life free of every hurt and hindrance. This is a book you will pick up and read over and over again, receiving something new and fresh from each reading.

—Prophet Cathy Lechner
Author and international speaker

At a time when many books are being written on "power, gifts, and the anointing," Jo Naughton addresses that which makes everything work in our life—the condition of our heart. When our heart is sick, so also is our whole person; without a doubt, we will feel the effects physically, emotionally, and spiritually. What Jo Naughton has done in writing this book is to provide a prescription for the soul from the Holy Spirit. It is therefore essential that the reader not only receive the specific medicine prescribed but also take the required dosage for each day. I believe the result will be a spiritually healthy heart—not just for those who are sick but also for all who desire spiritual health at a deeper level.

—Ken Gott
Partners in Harvest
Founder, House of Prayer Europe, Sunderland, England

In this life-changing book, *30-Day Detox for Your Soul*, Jo Naughton shares dynamic scriptural keys on how to remove the things from your life that hinder you spiritually—disappointment, worry, guilt, difficulty loving yourself, and more. Her step-by-step biblical approach also includes inspirational insights—such as discovering that love is the way, finding joy in serving, and experiencing "the test of time"—to enable you to build yourself up so that you may frame your future and unlock your destiny.

—*Dr. Steve L. Brock*
Well-known TV evangelist and Church of God bishop

Jo Naughton has written the most practical and insightful book on inner healing I've ever read. The blend of spiritual truths, insightful stories, and raw compassion moved me beyond words. I've ministered in over two thousand churches for more than forty-five years. This book should be taught in every church by ministers who have read it and have been healed by the Spirit through it. Jo, thank you for your vulnerability and transparency, which have brought healing and revelation to us all.

—*Bishop Duane Swilley*
Founder, A Place Called Hope Church/Avi's House Network

Wow! This is the book I've been looking for! It was intriguing all the way through. *30-Day Detox for Your Soul* is a manual to prepare you for your destiny. I know firsthand that if your negative memories are bigger than your dreams, you're going nowhere. Covering a broad range of issues that we all face, Jo Naughton skillfully shares the keys to dealing with life's difficulties—from disappointments and delays to setbacks and struggles with self-worth. This book is unique in the way Jo puts those keys in your hand and shows you how to use them. I loved how she included stories from her own life and from others' lives to validate her points. I'm giving this book to friends and colleagues to prepare them to rise above mediocrity, let go of the debilitating thoughts of the past, and establish a plan to succeed on purpose. It's easy to read and simple to apply. And, one month from now, you'll have a whole new approach to life. I seriously love this book!

—*Terri Savelle Foy*
Conference speaker, author, and success coach

It is my humble privilege and honor to acknowledge and attest this blessed book authored by Jo Naughton. Jo and her husband, Pastor Paul, are very dear friends of ours—in truth, they are like family with us in Christ Jesus. As the great Holy Spirit leads me to write these few lines as an endorsement of this precious, life-inspiring book, I lovingly encourage God's dear people to read and reread *30-Day Detox for Your Soul*. The Holy Spirit-inspired love of God and His truth imparted through this book will revive your life, giving you an abundance of peace, joy, healing, and wholeness. And, what's more, it will wipe away all your tears. As you go through this book, expect your miracle, and you will receive it all, in Jesus' name.

—*Rev. Dr. V. Dilkumar*
Founder and senior pastor, King's Revival Church Intl. Ministries, Dubai
(largest church in the Middle East)

Jo Naughton is a true "soul doctor." Her ministry has brought an outpouring of healing and deliverance to us in Ghana, West Africa. *30-Day Detox for Your Soul* is a heart-reviving book that will shine a light into your soul, bringing freedom and wholeness. It will inject new life into your relationship with God.

—*Prophet Nana Opoku-Sarkodie*
World Prayer Centre, Accra, Ghana

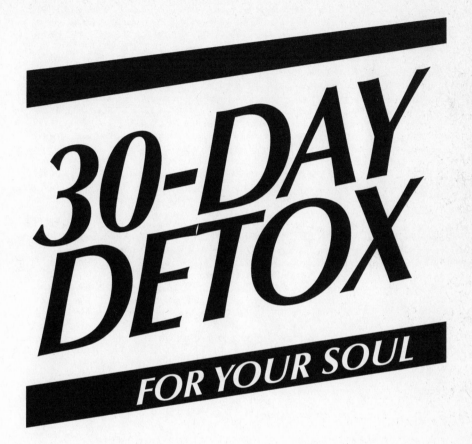

30-DAY DETOX

FOR YOUR SOUL

JO NAUGHTON

WHITAKER
HOUSE

Author's Note:
All names and some details have been changed to protect the identity of the people
whose stories are included in this book.

Unless otherwise indicated, all Scripture quotations are taken from the *New King James Version*, © 1979, 1980, 1982 by Thomas Nelson, Inc. Used by permission. All rights reserved. Scripture quotations marked (NIV) are taken from the *Holy Bible, New International Version*®, NIV®, © 1973, 1978, 1984, 2011 by Biblica, Inc.® Used by permission. All rights reserved worldwide. Scripture quotations marked (MSG) are taken from *The Message: The Bible in Contemporary Language* by Eugene H. Peterson, © 1993, 1994, 1995, 1996, 2000, 2001, 2002. Used by permission of NavPress Publishing Group. All rights reserved. Scripture quotations marked (AMP) are taken from *The Amplified*® *Bible*, © 1954, 1958, 1962, 1964, 1965, 1987 by The Lockman Foundation. Used by permission. (www.Lockman.org). Scripture quotations marked (NLT) are taken from the *Holy Bible, New Living Translation*, © 1996, 2004. Used by permission of Tyndale House Publishers, Inc., Carol Stream, Illinois 60188. All rights reserved. Scripture quotations marked (ESV) are taken from *The Holy Bible, English Standard Version*, © 2000, 2001, 1995 by Crossway Bibles, a division of Good News Publishers. Used by permission. All rights reserved. Scripture quotation marked (KJV) is taken from the King James Version of the Holy Bible. Scripture reference marked (NASB) refers to the updated *New American Standard Bible*®, NASB®, © 1960, 1962, 1963, 1968, 1971, 1972, 1973, 1975, 1977, 1995 by The Lockman Foundation. Used by permission. (www.Lockman.org).

Boldface type in the Scripture quotations indicates the author's emphasis.

Most definitions of Hebrew and Greek words are taken from *Strong's Exhaustive Concordance of the Bible*, referenced in the electronic Olive Tree NKJV Bible Study, © 2011 by Zondervan, or the *New Spirit-Filled Life Bible*, © 2002 by Thomas Nelson, Inc. Some definitions of Hebrew and Greek words are taken from *Strong's Talking Greek and Hebrew Dictionary* (© 2011 WORDsearch Bible Software, a division of LifeWay Christian Resources. Used by permission. All rights reserved.), the electronic version of the *New American Standard Exhaustive Concordance of the Bible*, (© 1981 by The Lockman Foundation. Used by permission. All rights reserved.), or *Vine's Complete Expository Dictionary of Old and New Testament Words*, VINE, (© 1985 by Thomas Nelson, Inc., Publishers, Nashville, TN. All rights reserved.).

30-Day Detox for Your Soul

Jo Naughton
www.jonaughton.com | jo@jonaughton.com

ISBN: 978-1-62911-341-8 • eBook ISBN: 978-1-62911-342-5
Printed in the United States of America | © 2015 by Jo Naughton

Whitaker House | 1030 Hunt Valley Circle | New Kensington, PA 15068
www.whitakerhouse.com

Library of Congress Cataloging-in-Publication Data
Naughton, Jo.
  30-day detox for your soul / by Jo Naughton.
    pages cm
  ISBN 978-1-62911-341-8 (trade pbk. : alk. paper) — ISBN 978-1-62911-342-5 (ebook)
1. Spiritual healing—Christianity. I. Title. II. Title: Thirty-day detox for your soul.
  BT732.5.N36 2015
  248.8'6—dc23

              2015007708

2 3 4 5 6 7 8 9 10 11 12 ⊔⊐ 23 22 21 20 19 18 17 16

This book is dedicated to my husband, Paul—my best friend, mentor, and greatest encourager.

Acknowledgements

Pastors Ken and Lois Gott:
Thank you for bringing the healing love of the Lord into my life.

Prophet Cathy Lechner:
Thank you for being a Grade A mama and mentor.

Apostle Guillermo Maldonado:
Thank you for bringing a greater measure of God's glory
into my ministry.

Tim Collins:
Thank you for investing your wisdom, time, and talents in this book.

Harvest Church London:
Thank you for being the best family a pastor could hope for.

Dad:
Thank you—I have learned more from you than you will ever know.

Mum:
Thank you for your prayers and support over the decades.

Contents

Foreword

It is a privilege for me to write this foreword to Pastor Jo Naughton's new book, *30-Day Detox for Your Soul*. She and her husband, Paul, pastor Harvest Church in London, England, a ministry that preaches the Word and demonstrates the supernatural power of God.

The personal journey that Jo has traveled, with its highs and lows, combined with her heart-piercing anointing to connect with people of all backgrounds and situations, enables her to shine a healing light in many people's lives, no matter what their circumstances.

Whether you've had a somewhat easy life or a very difficult one, God wants to deliver you from anything that keeps you from experiencing His joy and from becoming the complete person He created you to be—spirit, soul, and body. You were not meant to live with any amount of confusion, discouragement, or pain; you were created to live in an atmosphere of freedom and strength. Whether your hurts, doubts, insecurities, or fears are large or small, they will block you from fulfilling your destiny and manifesting the fullness of God's kingdom on earth. This book will speak straight to your heart, bringing healing and restoration.

We can receive true healing only in the presence of God, where His glory and power fill the atmosphere, reaching our hearts. In *30-Day Detox for Your Soul*, Jo Naughton guides you into God's presence each day so that you may be transformed and renewed, ready to enter into a whole new level of existence that you may not have imagined possible.

Pastor Jo is an anointed woman of great integrity, and I have seen firsthand how she loves the presence of God! Her experience in entering heaven's atmosphere and receiving God's supernatural touch will show you how to enter in and receive from Him, also. She demonstrates by example what it means to have honest, healing communion with God, knowing that *"the LORD is near to all who call upon Him, to all who call upon Him in truth"* (Psalm 145:18).

—*Apostle Guillermo Maldonado*

How to Do This Detox

Choose a time of day when you can do this detox for your soul. Perhaps early in the morning or before you go to bed at night is best for you. Set aside twenty minutes to read, to reflect, and to pray about each day's message. Have a Bible and a notebook at your side.

Try to keep your appointment with the Lord, but if you miss a day, don't become discouraged. Just pick up your book again when you can and carry on.

Each day has a specific theme based on a key verse from Proverbs, a book of the Bible that is God's timeless manual for life. There's also a "To Do Today" section—so, don't put off until tomorrow what you can do today! In addition, a prayer is provided to assist you in applying God's truths to your life and in developing your relationship with Him. And there's a suggested daily tweet. If you're on Twitter, you can share what God is doing in your life. You can also post the tweets as updates on Facebook. Doing so will strengthen your faith and, at the same time, encourage your friends.

You are about to embark on a glorious journey with Jesus. Open your heart, give Him your best, and watch what God will do!

—*Jo Naughton*

Step 1

OFF-LOAD

DAY 1

The Truth

"Buy the truth, and do not sell it."
—Proverbs 23:23

When you think about the human heart, what comes to mind? Is it love, relationships, and romance? Maybe you think of friends or family. Perhaps you remember heartache, betrayal, or grief. Maybe something else comes to mind. As we watch television or read magazines, it is easy for us to develop a skewed picture of what our hearts are really like. The Bible says that when God considers our hearts, one of His greatest concerns is our propensity for self-deception:

> *The heart is deceitful above all things, and desperately wicked; who can know it?* (Jeremiah 17:9)

This verse means that while the heart is capable of love, kindness, and compassion, it is also a master of deceit. We think we know ourselves. We think we know what is going on inside us. However, this Scripture indicates that, all too often, we don't.

Your heart is quite capable of pulling the wool over your eyes. Put simply, it can—and probably does—lie to you.

Home Truths

Several years ago, I discovered some home truths. A lady in our church told me that I was unapproachable. Another said she thought I was standoffish. A third person mentioned that she was once afraid to hug me. I was stunned. I thought of myself as a gentle lady, so this was a shock, and, to be honest, it was hurtful. I knew I was strong, but was I intimidating? Surely, that wasn't true, was it? I could have reacted like my friend's daughter who, when she was told off for slapping her sister, retorted, "It wasn't me—it was my hand!"

In this situation, it would have been easy to give in to self-pity: "I only ever have their best interests at heart. Why do I bother, anyway? It's not fair!" Unfortunately, feeling sorry for ourselves blinds us to the truth. I chatted it through with a close friend, who defended me, saying, "You're just very focused. You're a powerful woman of God—you don't need to change for anyone." It was tempting to believe that dear sister. After all, we can always find good excuses for our attitudes and our behaviors. I could even have blamed the women for being too timid. However, I knew that if I really wanted the Lord to use me, I would have to become someone whom others felt comfortable being with, and someone who overflowed with love. I knew that if I wanted to become my best, I would have to face the facts. God is truth, and He longs for us to be honest with Him and with ourselves:

> *Behold, You desire truth in the inward parts.* (Psalm 51:6)

The same David who wrote the above verse prayed that the Lord would search his heart and reveal its true contents. (See Psalm 139:23–24.) I asked God to change me, to make me gentler and kinder. The Lord never does a job by halves. He won't use a Band-Aid to treat a broken arm. So, He did not look at my symptoms alone. He addressed the cause and led me on a journey to the truth.

> *But when the Friend comes, the Spirit of the Truth, he will take you by the hand and guide you into all the truth.* (John 16:13 MSG)

I thought I knew myself: I was a happy, strong, and successful Christian woman. I had a wonderful family, a growing ministry, and a great job. Then the Spirit of Truth started to uncover old wounds. He revealed how hurts I'd experienced decades earlier were still affecting my day-to-day attitudes and reactions. Feelings of inadequacy that had set in during a difficult childhood had made me deeply insecure as an adult. I had gained a false sense of self-worth from promotion and position. I had become a status junkie. I cared too much what "important" people thought of me and needed regular reassurance from those closest to me. Facing the truth was hard, but it led me on a wonderful journey to healing and restoration. God went to the root of the issues and ministered to the hurts hidden deep inside me.

Revelation of Truth

We read in the book of Genesis that Isaac and his wife, Rebekah, had been trying to have a baby for twenty long years. When Rebekah eventually became pregnant with twins, things did not feel right to her. We don't know exactly what was wrong. She may have been in pain, or perhaps she felt an unpleasant squirming between the babies within her. Whatever was going on, she went to God in prayer and asked, *"If all is well, why am I like this?"* (Genesis 25:22).

I believe that is one of the most profound prayers in the Bible. Rather than ignoring that sinking feeling, or excusing that angst, why don't you do what Rebekah did and ask God why you are reacting the way you are? If, for example, you feel humiliated by experiences that others would merely brush off, or if you are overly sensitive, or if you are easily angered, ask God why. Just as He told Rebekah the cause of her inner turmoil, He will show you the things that need to be resolved within you.

Patrick was in full-time ministry when he reached rock bottom. His prayer life had become a daily struggle, and he felt as if God was unreachable, no matter how hard he tried to connect with Him. Despite this inner wilderness, Patrick lived life as though all was well. The Lord opened my eyes to the turmoil he was facing. I challenged him that it was time to be real. It is pointless giving the world (or, perhaps more accurately, the church) the impression that all is well when we are dying on the inside. Patrick got alone in his secret place of prayer and broke down. He stopped saying ritualistic prayers and instead got real with God. He told his heavenly Father about every failure and disappointment, and he soon found himself being refreshed in the presence of the Lord.

The former chief executive of one of the world's most successful retailers said, "Finding the truth was absolutely essential—it was the only way we could get out of the rut of being a middle-ranking [business]."* If we are happy with mediocrity, we don't need to know the truth. However, if we want to grow in God and to be our best, we must find out what about ourselves needs to change.

Facing Our Issues and Receiving Healing

The turmoil I had suffered while growing up had made me guarded as an adult. When life deals us difficult blows, we do what we can in order to cope and to recover. Then we adapt with the aim of protecting ourselves for the future. I had thought I was just "focused," but, in truth, I was prone to being harsh and abrupt. God's plan is that we face our issues and allow Him to heal our hurts. That way, we can be better, kinder, and more loving people.

When Rosie was just three years old, her parents went through a tumultuous divorce. Her dad had been repeatedly unfaithful, causing her mum to develop deep feelings of rejection. Her parents would argue night after night, with Rosie listening from the top of the stairs. Eventually, Rosie's mother moved out. With no money to raise her children, she left Rosie and her siblings with their father. He loved his girls and treated Rosie like a princess. Although her mum kept in touch, it was never the same.

Fast-forward to adult life. Rosie would often talk about her fantastic father who had showered her with affection. However, she never talked about her mother. Some friends assumed that was because the woman had passed away years earlier. One day, as I ministered to this dear lady, I told her that it was time to face the pain buried deep within her. She looked puzzled as I explained prophetically that God wanted to heal the rejection she felt in relation to her mother. Rosie had been in complete denial for decades about the wounds that were still unconsciously festering inside. Then the floodgates opened. Rosie cried before the Lord from the depths of her innermost being and told Him how much she had missed a mother's love.

---

* Terry Leahy, *Management in 10 Words* (London: Random House Business [an imprint of The Random House Group, Ltd.], 2012), 14.

God healed Rosie. She discovered an inner peace and security that she did not know even existed. She faced the truth, and God did the rest.

Perhaps you're frequently irritable or aloof. Maybe you're oversensitive, overambitious, or terribly shy. You're probably the product of your past. You have a choice: You can either live with your negative attitudes and feelings, making the excuse "That's just the way I am," or you can ask God to set you free. If you want to change, I encourage you to invite the Spirit of Truth into your heart.

The spirit of a man is the lamp of the LORD, searching all the inner depths of his heart. (Proverbs 20:27)

Our key Scripture for today says, *"Buy the truth, and do not sell it."* Truth has a price tag—it can be uncomfortable, and it can be painful. Sometimes, it is hard to acknowledge our shortcomings or to revisit the hurts of the past. However, if you're hungry for God's best, the price you will pay for truth cannot be compared to the rewards of a lifetime of greater peace and fulfillment.

TO DO TODAY

Consider your life experiences over the past few weeks or months. Have there been times when you have denied the truth or blamed others for your own failures? Write down any issues that you know you need to face and then ask God to start a new work in your heart and life.

PRAYER

Dear Lord,

I invite the Spirit of Truth to come into my heart. I welcome You, and I'm ready for the truth. I'm sorry for pointing the finger at others and blaming them for my shortcomings when I should have taken responsibility for my errors. Please become my closest, most trusted Friend. I know You will lead me with care and love. Reveal any issues within me that You want to deal with, and any wounds that You desire to heal. I won't dig about for "junk" to pull up from my past, but I will pray about anything that You bring to my consciousness. I won't ignore the truth; I will face the facts, because You are ready to heal me and to change me. I ask You to lead me into a deeper and richer relationship with You. In Jesus' name, amen.

TODAY'S TWEET:

Truth has a price & I'm willing to pay it. #detoxforyoursoul

DAY 2

Dealing with Disappointment

"Hope deferred makes the heart sick."
—Proverbs 13:12

After our son was born, I was desperate for a second child. I had lost a daughter before his arrival, so I felt I should already be a mother of two. After some delay, I was overjoyed to discover that I was pregnant again. All went well until one Sunday morning while I was getting ready for church. I started to miscarry, and it was heartbreaking. I had been carrying the promise of a happy family, and now my baby was gone. I had to start the painful process of trying again.

"Waiting" often sounds harmless, but sometimes it hurts. We want to have *now* what the future holds. Maybe you are believing for a baby or waiting for your future spouse to come into your life. Perhaps you have been desperately praying for a new job or a promotion. You may be standing in faith for healing for yourself or for someone you dearly love. Or you could be waiting for a different type of breakthrough in your circumstances, or a turnaround in your life. When something is terribly important to us, it can be painful to be patient about receiving it.

Our idea of "a little while" is very different from God's. To Him, a day is like a thousand years. (See 2 Peter 3:8.) And while you're waiting, perhaps—like me—you've felt like reminding God that you are a mere mortal and that time down here drags! The wait sometimes makes our hearts grow weary. As excitement fades and determination alone keeps us going, we can feel disheartened. *The Message* Bible puts today's key verse like this: *"Unrelenting disappointment leaves you heartsick."* Perhaps that is your story: one setback after another. Or you may have waited a very long time for an important answer. Such experiences can leave us heavyhearted and despondent, even depressed.

Give Your Disappointment to God as an Offering

Discouragement is debilitating, and it can be dangerous. When we are disheartened or heavyhearted, we feel like giving up on our dreams, and we easily drift away from God's Word and from prayer. In addition, we can become spiritually vulnerable. The Bible teaches us to exchange our sickness for God's health. (See, for example, Isaiah 53:5.) It teaches us to resist the devil (see James 4:7) and to cast our cares onto the Lord (see 1 Peter 5:7). However, it is not clear about what we should do with disappointment. So, I asked the Lord about it. He told me that we should give disappointment to Him as an offering.

The first part of the giving is letting it out. We need to tell the Lord, out loud, how we feel.

Pour out your heart like water before the face of the Lord.
(Lamentations 2:19)

After I miscarried, I went to God in prayer and told Him the truth about how I felt. I expressed how much it hurt; I explained that I could not understand why it had happened. I had already lost one child, so, to have a miscarriage just eighteen months later felt so unfair. I poured out my heart, and I asked Him to heal me. As children describe their sadnesses in detail to their fathers and mothers, I told the Lord exactly what was going on in my heart. I poured out my pain before Him.

I encourage you to do the same if you are down or disheartened. If you are tired and weary, go into your secret place and talk to God about it. Tell Him if you thought things would have changed by now. Tell Him if you feel let down or forgotten. Tell Him if you are disappointed.

If you are a parent, you will no doubt cherish the times when your children tell you about the things that are really bothering them. So, too, your heavenly Father loves it when you share your innermost feelings with Him.

The second step of giving our disappointment to the Lord is leaving it with Him. That's what makes it an offering. All too often, we think we have a right to feel the way we do—disheartened, discouraged, and so on. As a result, it can be hard for us to let go of our pains. While we hang on to disappointment, it will weigh us down. Yet, when we leave it with the Lord because we trust Him, we will feel relieved. Again and again in the Psalms, David prayed, "I put my trust in You." (See, for example, Psalm 7:1; 25:20; 31:1) In other words, whenever his soul started to wander, David would put his trust in God—or he would renew his trust.

Jesus said,

Come to me, all you who are weary and burdened, and I will give you rest.   (Matthew 11:28 NIV)

Disappointment opens the door to the spirit of heaviness, which can, in turn, lead to depression. It is therefore very important that we learn to leave disappointment with the Lord. It is like laying down a heavy load. God wants to give you rest. His rest will refresh, restore, and rejuvenate your soul.

Let's look at Matthew 11:28 in *The Amplified Bible*:

Come to Me, all you who labor and are heavy-laden and overburdened, and I will cause you to rest. [I will ease and relieve and refresh your souls.]

The breakthrough you need will come from your being in the presence of God. As you draw near to Him, He will draw near to you. (See James 4:8.) As you pour out your heart before Him—no matter how big or small the issue—He will hear you and relieve you of your burdens. Enjoying the wonderful favor of God is just what we need when we are downhearted:

When the king smiles, there is life; his favor refreshes like a spring rain.   (Proverbs 16:15 NLT)

A Setback—or a Setup for Success?

David went through a terrible trial at a place called Ziklag. After ten years on the run from King Saul, he was eventually given Ziklag by the Philistines as his own city. It was a safe haven for David and his men, a place that he and his family could call home. Then, one day, when David and his warriors returned from war, they discovered that their beloved Ziklag had been burned to the ground. Not only that, but every man's wife and children had been taken captive, and his belongings had been stolen. Just when David had thought that life was looking up, everything around him crashed to the ground. He was devastated. It would have been easy for him to have given up on his dreams. Instead, he poured out his heart before the Lord, giving God his pain, and then he asked for instructions. He would not allow disappointment to hold him back. He laid it down and looked to the Lord for deliverance. The result was that not only did David and his men recover everything they had lost, but, in less than one week, David was also crowned king of Judah. Just a few days after David's greatest disappointment, he stepped into the fulfillment of his destiny.

Remember that sometimes a setback is actually a setup for success. In God, delay is not denial. Just because it has taken longer than you expected does not mean it isn't coming. Even if you are disappointed because what you'd hoped for came to nothing, remember that God is faithful. Sometimes, the most important breakthroughs in life come after a difficult journey. The longer the wait or the harder the trial, the sweeter the success.

The second part of our key verse in Proverbs tells us the end of the story:

> *Hope deferred makes the heart sick,* **but** *a dream fulfilled is a tree of life.*   (Proverbs 13:12 NLT)

Consider these biblical examples: Abraham waited twenty-five years before his miracle baby was born. Joseph endured thirteen years of slavery and prison, but he went on to become the equivalent of prime minister of Egypt. Moses seemed to be out of the picture of God's plan for forty years, but, at the age of eighty, he led all the Israelites out of Egyptian slavery.

Good things come to those who wait. When God is in control, destiny will be fulfilled at the right time.

TO DO TODAY

Are you feeling disappointed? Is there something you have been hoping for that is taking far longer to be fulfilled than you ever expected? Have you experienced one letdown after another? Perhaps you are weary because you have been waiting for a long time. It is OK to be real with God about your feelings of disappointment. In fact, doing so is essential. He already knows how you feel. If you are fed up, disheartened, or overwhelmed, it is probably time to be honest about that fact. Get a piece of paper and write down every source of your sadness. Go into as much detail as possible, asking the Holy Spirit to enable you to remember clearly. Then, tell the Lord everything that has weighed you down, and give your disappointments to Him as an offering.

PRAYER

Father God,

I have been waiting for a long time for Your Word to be fulfilled in my life. I have been hurt by disappointments and delays. I'm tired. I kept thinking that the fulfillment would come "this month" or "this year," but here I am, still waiting. [*Be specific about your experiences. For example, if you have suffered a loss, express that loss to the Lord.*] I give all my disappointments to You now, Lord. I give every source of sadness and weariness to You, because You care about me. I am Your child, and my future is in Your hands. Once again, I put my trust in You. I draw near to You, and I thank You that You are drawing near to me, too. I thank You for Your precious presence. I receive Your healing and Your refreshing rain. I know that You are faithful. In Jesus' name, amen.

TODAY'S TWEET:

Delay is not denial. #detoxforyoursoul

DAY 3

Pain Relief

"Laughter can conceal a heavy heart,
but when the laughter ends, the grief remains."
—Proverbs 14:13 (NLT)

A painful put-down at work, the cold shoulder from a person you deeply admire, a hurtful betrayal by a brother or sister, or an outright rejection from someone you love—life can deal hard blows, and the pain can be debilitating. Proverbs 15:13 (MSG) says, *"A sad heart makes it hard to get through the day."* Like a punch to the gut, it can leave us reeling. It can drain our strength so that we're running on empty. We carry around sadness in our soul.

Most of us get hurt on a regular basis. We normally swallow the pain, brush ourselves off, toughen up, and then carry on. We may know how to hide our hurt, but that does not stop it from causing us harm:

By sorrow of the heart the spirit is broken. (Proverbs 15:13)

In the above verse, the Hebrew word translated *"sorrow"* can refer to any type of pain, wound, or emotional injury. The word for *"heart"* refers to our inner thoughts and feelings. And another meaning of the word translated *"spirit"* is "breath." Any sadness left lingering in our hearts can choke the very life out of us. After the pain has been numbed, we can end up feeling dry and detached. Our relationship with the Lord can be damaged, because we commune with Him from our hearts—from the very place where we are wounded.

You may have been wondering why you are in a spiritual wilderness. You serve God, study His Word, and spend time in prayer. However, you feel empty and disheartened. I encourage you to ask God if you have any unhealed hurts. You may need to face some buried pain so that you can encounter the Lord's wonderful healing power.

Unresolved Pain and Hidden Wounds

Fractured relationships can be particularly hard to bear. Misunderstandings, unkindnesses, broken promises, and neglect can harm even the strongest man or woman. Most of the time, we feel unable to share our difficulties with anyone, so, instead, we ignore our pain and try to move on. When things improve (if they do), the past may be forgotten, but the wounds may still fester beneath the surface.

If we have unresolved pain deep within us, we become more defensive toward other people. Suppose you gashed your leg, but the wound only partially healed. It would be agony if someone bumped the affected area. In the same way, if we have unhealed hearts, even people's teasing and jokes might provoke a negative reaction from us. We might be oversensitive or quick to build walls of isolation. Inevitably, we will end up wounding those closest to us, because hurt people tend to hurt other people.

We must realize that, from time to time, we all need pain relief for our souls. This will protect others as well as ourselves. When my cousin was in labor, she was not given enough anesthetic and oxygen to relieve her pain. She was in such agony that she wrapped her arms tightly around her husband's neck and held him in a headlock while screeching at the top of her voice. Once the baby was born, her husband was the one who ended up in the emergency room!

A broken spirit saps a person's strength. (Proverbs 17:22 NLT)

Early on in our ministry, my husband and I went through an upsetting trial. Accusations of impropriety were fired at us by an influential person. Close friends distanced themselves from us, and people who had once admired us avoided eye contact with us. Not one of the allegations was true, but God told us not to try to defend ourselves. I was hurt by what had been said, by the way it had been said, and by who had said it. On the night that it all blew up, I went to bed crushed and confused. It felt as though someone had fired a dart straight into my heart. I was due to minister a day or two later, so I knew I needed God's help—and quickly. The Holy Spirit brought this Scripture to mind:

Who can bear a broken spirit?   (Proverbs 18:14)

I realized that something deep within me was broken. I couldn't bear the pain. Getting out of bed, I knelt down and called out to the Lord, "I can't carry on while my heart is hurting so badly." I cried in His presence and told Him what had pained me the most. As I poured out my heart before God, He tended to my wounds. I felt the pain dislodge. I went to bed tired but relieved. I slept soundly and woke up the next morning at peace. The storm continued, yet I walked through it. God has a way of turning trials into testimonies. Within two months, God supernaturally revealed the truth, and we were entirely vindicated.

The Master Restorer

We need to treat emotional injury as we would any other wound. If I were to break my leg, I would not hesitate to get medical help. The main difference is that, in most cases, a doctor can't heal a hurting heart. You and I need to go straight to the heavenly Father with our pain. He is the Master Restorer. As Jacob said,

Let us arise and go up to Bethel; and I will make an altar there to God, who answered me in the day of my distress and has been with me in the way which I have gone.   (Genesis 35:3)

Tom was a successful trainer who was married with three children. On the surface, everything in his life seemed to be fine. However, he was domineering and aggressive—especially toward those closest to him. His wife and children walked on eggshells around him and dreaded the thought of any outbursts from him.

Tom was in a meeting one day when the Holy Spirit took him back to a terrible trauma that he had suffered when he was just twelve years of age. He had been raped by someone who was supposed to be protecting him. Pain and shame, which Tom had buried deep within, came flooding back, and he poured out his heart before the Lord. He laid down a heavy burden that he had been carrying around all his life. This release became the beginning of an extraordinary transformation. As God worked within him, Tom became a loving husband, a kind father, and a compassionate church leader whose ministry is now international.

Perhaps you have never before asked the Lord to heal your heart. I suggest that you start going to Him whenever you are wounded. It does not matter whether you've been hurt by a major trauma or by just the normal ups and downs of life. You need to ask the Lord to take away your pain so that you can be free to live life to the full. Maybe you seek God's healing only occasionally, such as when you are at a conference or in a big meeting at a church. There is no reason to wait. Bring every hurt to Him as soon as it happens.

The Bible tells us to come to Jesus like a little child. (See, for example, Matthew 19:13–15.) Children know how to let out their pain. When my daughter was young, if something upset her, she would run straight into my arms and tell me what had happened. She would recount who did what and how it made her feel. Within a few moments, her tears dried up, and she enjoyed a reassuring cuddle with me. We must learn to become like a child in this way. We need to tell God how we have been hurt. The following Scripture will help us further in regard to this process:

> Trust in Him at all times, you people; pour out your heart before Him; God is a refuge for us.   (Psalm 62:8)

Many of us have had our trust broken at some point. I assure you, you *can* trust the Lord. You can share your deepest secrets and your most private thoughts with Him. He will not be shocked or offended. Again, He already knows them, anyway. However, by telling Him, you will use your mouth as a trigger to release the hurt and to draw near to God.

TO DO TODAY

Are you carrying around any emotional pain? Do you have certain memories that still make you wince? Have you had hurtful experiences that you don't like to recall? Perhaps something from your past has come to the surface while you have been reading this book. If not, I suggest that you ask the Lord to bring any unhealed wounds to your remembrance so that you can deal with them. Then take them to the Master Restorer in prayer. He will bring relief and will restore your peace.

PRAYER

Father God,

Negative things have happened to me that have deeply impacted me. The bad experiences of the past have affected my life today, and I want to be free from them. [*Don't just tell God that you were "hurt." Tell Him, out loud, exactly what happened—even the little details. Imagine that you are back in that situation, and tell the Lord how it all made you feel. Open your heart to Him, describing every hurt and revealing every question that you are holding inside.*]

Your Word says that You heal the brokenhearted. I ask that Your healing power will flow into my soul right now. Come and restore me. I open my heart and invite You into the painful memories that I have buried deep within. Jesus, You are a Miracle Worker, and I put my faith in Your ability to make me whole. In Jesus' name, amen.

TODAY'S TWEET:

Hurt people hurt other people. Healed people bring healing. #detoxforyoursoul

DAY 4

I Have a Father

"My [child], *hear the instruction of your father."*
—Proverbs 1:8

A friend once asked a group of five-year-olds to draw God. Some painted an old fellow up in the clouds. A few sketched men wearing suits
who resembled their fathers. One child left the page blank. When quizzed,
the little girl explained, "I don't have a dad, so I don't know what God looks
like."

Most people grow up believing that God is just like their father. If you
were the apple of your dad's eye, you will probably find it easy to receive love
from the Lord. However, if your father broke his promises or abandoned
the family, you might think that God will let you down, too. If your dad
was stingy, you may have difficulty accepting that the Lord really wants
to bless you. If your dad was harsh, you might think that God is harsh, as
well. If you have never had a father figure in your life, you may struggle to
relate to your heavenly Father at all.

Even if you enjoyed a generally happy home life while you were growing up, I am guessing that your parents weren't perfect. They might have
been overbearing or distant. They might have argued with you or expected
too much from you. Perhaps work or ministry commitments frequently
kept them away from home. Our view of God can be influenced by such
experiences.

Knowing God as Our Loving Father

The entire book of Proverbs is written to sons (and daughters). It is not written to followers or servants. In the *New King James Version*, the readers of Proverbs are addressed as *"children"* four times and as *"son"* twenty-five times, such as in the following verse.

My son, pay attention to my wisdom; lend your ear to my understanding.... (Proverbs 5:1)

My husband, Paul, is a wonderful father to our children, Ben and Abby. Of course, he misses the mark from time to time, but when he does, he is quick to say he is sorry. On one such occasion, when our son was just four years old, my husband knelt down before our little boy as he apologized. Paul asked Ben to pray for him to be a better daddy next time. Immediately, Ben laid his hands on his dad's head and shouted at the top of his voice, "I rebuke that spirit of anger, in Jesus' name!" Everybody laughed—but my husband was instantly delivered!

To thrive in God, we need to know Him as Father. And not just any father but the truly wonderful Dad that He is. God is not a man, so He never makes mistakes, as we do. He is completely trustworthy. He is love, so He is exceptionally patient and wonderfully kind. Before Jesus lifted a finger in ministry, God the Father told Him loud and clear that He loved Him. In essence, the Father's love was not based on Jesus' obedience or performance. He loved Jesus (and still does) just because He was (and is) His Son.

This is my dearly loved Son, who brings me great joy. (Matthew 3:17 NLT)

When you accept Jesus as your Lord and Savior, the heavenly Father adopts you as His own. You belong to the best family in the world. You have a Father who will never fail you and will never leave you. He loves you, not because of what you can do but because of who you are.

But as many as received Him, to them He gave the right to become children of God. (John 1:12)

I love my children. I enjoy watching them chat with their friends, concentrate on problems, ride their bikes, and even sleep. God's love for you is much more wonderful than that. He is interested in you and takes pleasure in you. He loves you because you are you and because you are His.

See what [an incredible] quality of love the Father has given (shown, bestowed on) us, that we should [be permitted to] be named and called and counted the children of God! And so we are! (1 John 3:1 AMP)

If you had a difficult or nonexistent relationship with your father, I encourage you to meditate on the above verse. The Lord wants to lavish His love on you and to heal you of the pain of the past. When we have been rejected or mistreated by our natural dads, we need to face our pain and ask God to heal us deep down.

Derek's father was repeatedly unfaithful to his wife, Derek's mother. When Derek was just eight years old, he would wait up night after night with his mum for his dad to return home from his numerous affairs. Sent to bed when his dad got back, he would lie awake in bed, burying his head under his pillow and trying not to listen to the angry arguments that reverberated around the house. After his parents divorced, Derek and his brother were sent to live with strangers. Things went from bad to worse when their mum remarried six months later. Derek eventually ran away from home.

After giving his life to the Lord as an adult, Derek sought to honor his father and his mother. He helped his mum as much as he could and nursed his dad until the day of his death. Yet, deep inside, he was still full of bitterness and pain. His parents never told him that they loved him. They never acknowledged the hurt that they had caused him.

Decades later, Derek was in a meeting in Florida where I was ministering about fathers. He responded to the altar call for prayer, and, as the Spirit of God touched him, he began to weep from the depths of his being. Pain that had been buried for fifty-four years was released, and the healing love of God poured into his heart. As the ministry time ended, Derek felt a freedom that he hadn't known was possible. Joy filled his soul. Even his wife saw a difference; she said that she had gained a new, happier husband from that day forth.

Your Heavenly Father, Your Refuge

I do not know what your relationship with your dad was like. However, I do know that God wants to heal all your pain. When we face the truth about the mistakes our parents made, we are not dishonoring them. We are simply acknowledging that our family was not perfect. When we are real, we make a way for the Lord to heal us. I encourage you to open your heart and tell God about the things your father or mother did (or did not do) that caused you pain or sadness. When we tell Him our hurts, He can heal us. Soon, you will find that your view of your heavenly Father is changing. It will be easier for you to receive His love. Again, the truth is that God loves you for who you are. He loves you completely, and He accepts you. He chose to adopt you as His own. Even if you had a great dad, you need to know that your heavenly Father is more wonderful still.

> *The eternal God is your refuge, and his everlasting arms are under*
> *you.* (Deuteronomy 33:27 NLT)

A "refuge" is a safe place. It is somewhere you can unwind, relax, and be yourself. Your Father is your refuge, and His arms are outstretched toward you. Just as the young man in the parable of the prodigal son enjoyed a wonderful hug when he returned to his father, so God is waiting with open arms for you. The Bible says that the father ran to meet his wayward son:

> *But while he was still a long way off, his father saw him and was moved*
> *with pity and tenderness [for him]; and he ran and embraced him and*
> *kissed him [fervently].* (Luke 15:20 AMP)

When I first called the Lord "Daddy God," it changed my relationship with Him. It brought me closer to Him. The Lord is your Daddy, too. He loves you and has a tender heart toward you. He wants you to enjoy the reassurance and security that come from knowing that you are loved by your heavenly Father. In the book of Proverbs, the reader is not simply referred to as "*son*" or "*child*" but as "*my son*" or "*my child*." (See, for example,

Proverbs 1:8 NKJV, NLT.) You are not an outsider. You are not an intruder or a fraud. You are the real thing—a son or daughter of the Most High God.

TO DO TODAY

Write down four or five impressions that you feel in your heart when you think about your earthly father, even if you don't know him. If this exercise has brought buried emotions to the surface, pour out your pain before the Lord and ask Him to heal your heart. Then ask yourself if your impressions of your earthly father have affected your view of God—for good or for ill. When you are ready, go to God in prayer with your conclusions.

PRAYER

Father God,

I thank You that You love me. There is nothing I can do to make You love me more, and there is nothing I can do to make You love me less. You love me completely and perfectly.

[If you have had a difficult relationship with your dad, continue by using this paragraph:]

I was hurt by my dad, and I think it has negatively affected my view of You. [*Express to the Lord what your relationship with your dad was like. Be specific. Tell God about your pain and how it made you feel back then, as well as how you feel now. Then ask Him to heal your heart and to restore you.*] I know that You are different from my dad. Although he was [*name his shortcomings that particularly affected you*], You want the best for me. I thank You that You love me just as You love Jesus. You are not like human beings. You won't let me down. You are patient with me, and You will always be kind to me. I receive Your love afresh today.

[If you have had a good relationship with your dad, continue by using this paragraph:]

Thank You for my dad. Thank You that I have seen some of what You are like through him. However, I know that You are the greatest Father a child could have. I ask You to reveal Your Father-heart to me in greater measure.

[Conclude with this:]

I thank You that when I made Jesus my Lord and Savior, You received me as Your very own child; You adopted me. You accept me, and You cherish me. Lord, I receive Your love today. I see Your everlasting arms wrapped around me. I thank You that I am safe and secure when I am with You. You are my Daddy God, and I am Your own child. In Jesus' name, amen.

TODAY'S TWEET:

I'm going to get to know my heavenly Father. #detoxforyoursoul

DAY 5

Do You Like Yourself?

"As in water face reflects face, so a man's heart reveals the man."
—Proverbs 27:19

My self-image is the picture I have of myself. It is what I think of me. It will determine my thoughts, my attitudes, and my behavior. It will influence who I become. So, it is important that my view of myself is a healthy one. For many years, I had no problem *loving* myself. After all, God loves me. However, I struggled to *like* myself. I thought I was efficient, focused, and well organized but not really very likeable. I knew that if I wanted to fulfill my destiny, I needed to be my best. But if I had a negative self-image, it would hold me back and hinder the work of God through me. So, I asked God to show me why I didn't like me. I was surprised by what He revealed.

Although I had been healed of childhood hurts many years earlier, one hidden sadness remained: I had been quite an unpopular child. I had friends, but they often found me annoying, loud, or a bit of a bother. I was sometimes left out of games because I would spoil the fun. On one occasion, I paid a boy five pence (ten cents) just to walk home with me. I formed a deep, subconscious view that I wasn't a very nice girl. I believed that I was someone whom other children only tolerated. In their patience, they merely put up with me.

Although I went on to be pretty successful by the world's standards, that self-image stayed deep within me well into my forties. If you had asked me if my husband or my close friends liked me, I would have said, "Of course!" However, if you had asked me if they were *right* to like me, I would have faltered.

What do you think of yourself? You may be very sure of your strengths and feel confident in your gifts, but do you like *you*? Would you choose yourself as a friend? I hope you know that God loves you. Do you think He likes you, too?

Self-image is forged at a young age. Whether you acknowledge it or not, your view of yourself has shaped your life and will continue to shape it. For example, if you were called "four eyes," "fatty," "loudmouth," or "stupid," those names may have affected your identity. If you were betrayed or rejected by friends or family, those experiences have likely framed your self-image.

Bullying can be particularly debilitating to a healthy identity. It can squash even strong souls, leaving them feeling that they are constantly living life a step below other people. Perhaps your teachers hurled abuse at you during Sports Day at your school, or you were humiliated as you limped in last in a race as the whole school looked on. Maybe you were always excluded when teams were chosen. It is extraordinary the lasting impact that childhood experiences can have on our view of ourselves.

Our God Mends Broken Things

You might be wondering what you can do about all of this now. Or you might think that your life is fine and you don't need any healing. However, if your self-image is damaged, it will hamper your progress. We serve a healing God who is in the business of mending broken things.

Meg wanted to become a prefect in her final year at primary school. When she approached her teacher about it, she was informed in no uncertain terms that it was not even a possibility. "Staff at school just don't like you," she was told. The rejection winded her. She moved on to the remainder of her schooling with one aim: to be appreciated by teachers. Over the next seven years, Meg worked hard to please people and eventually achieved her ambition of being appointed head girl. She had a medal to prove her popularity, and the events at school defined her personality. Wherever she went, she strived for recognition and appreciation. As long as she was affirmed, all was well.

Meg attended a conference where I ministered about how certain experiences can mark our lives. She broke. The Holy Spirit took her back to that experience in primary school and healed her of the rejection she had suffered so long ago. The results amazed her. She felt like a new person: confident, relaxed, and free to be herself.

God wants to rebuild your inner reflection. He wants you to like yourself just as much as He likes you. He is your loving Father, and He desires that you be whole—inside and out. Think about God's incredible love for you. He chose you before He even started making the earth: *"He chose us in Him before the foundation of the world"* (Ephesians 1:4). God designed you. He shaped your personality, created your face and hair, and chose your height. When He was finished, He was delighted. David wrote,

You formed my inward parts; You covered me in my mother's womb. I will praise You, for I am fearfully and wonderfully made; marvelous are Your works, and that my soul knows very well.

(Psalm 139:13–14)

As you have progressed through life, God has seen your happiness and your sadness. Now He wants to bring you wholeness. You need to know that He loves you *and* likes you. You are His creation, His child, and His friend.

See what [an incredible] quality of love the Father has given (shown, bestowed on) us, that we should [be permitted to] be named and called and counted the children of God! And so we are! (1 John 3:1 AMP)

I remember hearing the story of a biological son and an adopted son in the same family who argued over who their father loved the most. Jimmy, the natural son, said, "I know Daddy loves me more than he loves you, because I'm his *real* child." Tears welled up in Johnny's eyes until he had a flash of inspiration: "Daddy *had* to have you, but he *chose* me!" That's who we are: chosen and adopted, accepted for who we are. Psalm 139 shows the depths of God's knowledge of us.

God knows what makes you tick. He knows what irritates and angers you. He knows when your motives are right and when they are wrong. He knows when you are being unkind or greedy. He knows what makes you laugh and what makes you cry. In fact, the Lord knows everything there is to know about you. With all His understanding about every attribute that makes you uniquely you, He loves you unconditionally and accepts you completely. It is not that He doesn't care about your defects; it is just that He loves you in spite of them.

King David became one of Israel's greatest leaders. I believe that a healed self-image helped to make this possible. Although David was not his father's favorite (see 1 Samuel 16:10–11), he knew deep inside that he was wonderful in God's eyes. The put-downs and low opinions of his brothers (see 1 Samuel 17:26–28) did not matter to him because he was convinced that the God of all the earth thought he was marvelous. Look at this verse from Psalm 139 again:

> *I am fearfully and wonderfully made; marvelous are Your works, and that my soul knows very well.* (Psalm 139:14)

God the Father loves you, just as He loved David. He treasures you, just as He treasures Jesus. Allow those thoughts to sink in. You were made by God on purpose. You were a brilliant idea, and you are a marvelous creation. The King of Kings doesn't have any "off" days. You were created by the Master in His prime, and He was (and is) pleased. Again, at the very outset of Jesus' ministry, before He preached a single message or healed any sick people, God affirmed His Son with His love. Our heavenly Father told His Son that He was delighted with Him. And, you and I are "*joint heirs with Christ*" (Romans 8:17). The love that God has for us is just as perfect as the love He has for Jesus.

What am I saying? Just as God spoke words of love and affirmation over Jesus, so the Lord wants you to speak the same words of reassurance to yourself. Picture God the Father standing before you with open arms, and hear Him say, "You are my well-loved child, and, in you, I am well pleased." (See, for example, Matthew 3:17.)

TO DO TODAY

Philemon 1:6 shows us the importance of acknowledging the good that is within us. Write down five things about yourself that you like. Then jot down five things that you don't like. If you struggle to see the good in yourself, ask God to show you what He likes about you. If you find that the bad things about yourself make you recoil, ask Him to heal your self-image.

PRAYER

Lord God,

I have sometimes struggled to like myself. Various experiences in life have affected my self-image. [*If particular events, circumstances, or labels have wounded your inner image, tell the Lord about them. Explain what happened and how it made you feel. Ask Him to heal you.*] I ask You to mend my self-image. Restore my view of myself so that I see what You see. You chose me, You planned me, You knitted me together in my mother's womb, and You rejoiced when I was born. You love me on my good days and on my bad days. You love me because I am Yours. I know that as my self-image is restored, my life will reflect Your love and Your goodness more and more. I give you all the praise! In Jesus' name, amen.

TODAY'S TWEET:

My new self-image in God will help to shape my new destiny. #detoxforyoursoul

DAY 6

Words That Hurt

"There is one who speaks like the piercings of a sword."
—Proverbs 12:18

Words are powerful. God spoke the world into existence. Whatever He said came into being. The sun, the moon, the mountains, the animals, and the birds were all created by God's words. We human beings are made in His image (see Genesis 1:26–27), and our speech is powerful, too. God's plan was that our conversation would encourage others, bring healing, and convey love. Unfortunately, all too often, our words cause others pain.

Today's key verse compares certain words to a sword. A sword is a weapon used to injure and even to kill. It is amazing how much damage speech can do, too. Words are one of the enemy's most trusted weapons. Satan uses what the Bible calls *"fiery darts"* (Ephesians 6:16) to destroy people's dreams, to damage relationships, to discourage, and to humiliate. I remember describing my vision to a Christian leader many years ago. I was sure she would share my excitement. Instead, she shrugged her shoulders, wrinkled her nose, and said, "You can't do that." I was gutted. Because I was insecure, her words squashed me and made me feel embarrassed about my dreams.

The Power of Words

Most of us are accustomed to fending off unpleasant comments or painful remarks. The darts pierce us, and we're hurt. The wind is knocked out of us, and our excitement diminishes. But we try our best to carry on despite the pain. We put the past to one side and move on.

If someone were to stab you with a knife, you would rush to the nearest hospital emergency room for immediate treatment. Well, your emotional heart is even more important than your body! You were not designed merely to "just get by" and survive. You were created to thrive. When someone wounds you with his or her words, you need healing so that you can be your best. Jesus said,

> A thief is only there to steal and kill and destroy. I came so they can have real and eternal life, more and better life than they ever dreamed of.   (John 10:10 MSG)

Satan came to steal your faith, to kill your joy, and to destroy your destiny. He often uses cutting remarks, spoken by people around us, to carry out this dirty work. By contrast, Jesus wants you to enjoy your life. He wants you to fulfill your God-given potential. And, to live in fullness, you need to deal with the effects of negative words spoken against you.

In the Old Testament, Jacob recognized the power of words. At a time when people understood the importance of names, Jacob's father called him "Deceiver." That's what the name *Jacob* means. So, every time his dad called him by name, it was as if he was shouting, "Hey, Cheat!" Yet, in His great love, God took away the shame of Jacob's demeaning name and instead called him Israel, which means "Prince with God." It was *Israel* whom God named His nation after, not *Jacob*.

Rachel, Jacob's dearly loved wife, named their last-born son *Ben-Oni*, meaning "Son of My Sorrow." Jacob overruled her decision and instead called him *Benjamin*, which means "Son of my Right Hand." Jacob did not want his son to suffer from the stigma and hurt of a cruel name.

"Cutting Words Wound"

Ask the Holy Spirit to help you remember words that have hurt you. Consider your most important relationships. Have you been wounded by any harsh or thoughtless words by those closest to you? Perhaps you were bullied or called cruel names when you were growing up. Were your friends critical of you when you had a disagreement with them? Maybe your spouse said something spiteful to you in the heat of an argument. Perhaps certain people have said unkind things to you; afterward, they may have said they were sorry, but their words still penetrated your heart. Sometimes, people don't mean to hurt us, yet, as we have seen, because of our existing insecurities, even harmless comments by others can cause us injury.

Was a leader abrupt toward you, or was a colleague harsh with you? When dismissive or negative remarks are made toward us by a mother figure or a father figure, they can have a particularly harmful effect. God intended that parents should speak life and confidence to their children. So, when authority figures get it wrong, we can be deeply wounded—even crushed.

> *Kind words heal and help; cutting words wound and maim.*
> (Proverbs 15:4 MSG)

Freedom from Destructive Words

Every word that hurts us is like the piercing of a dart. The ferocity of the attack and the vulnerability of the victim determine the depth of the wound. In *The Message* Bible, our key verse reads, *"Rash language cuts and maims"* (Proverbs 12:18). Indeed, careless words can be crippling. If you have been crushed by unkind comments, it is very important for you to ask God to heal you. You might not have been brokenhearted over those comments, but the words might have caused you to feel disheartened or discouraged. That is still the work of the enemy, and you need to be set free to dream and to believe once again.

> *Death and life are in the power of the tongue.*   (Proverbs 18:21)

Have you ever wondered why the word *"death"* comes before *"life"* in this verse? I believe it is because the tongue is used for destruction more often than it is used for its original purpose of construction. Consider what other people have said about your abilities, your work, or your looks. My junior high teacher used to call me "Funny Face" and "Rubber Lips," although I don't think I had either (no contradictory e-mails, please!). Has anyone ever told you that you were a bad husband or wife, an awful father or mother, a useless teacher, or a poor leader? Maybe someone has called you "stupid" or "fool." Perhaps you have been told you were ugly or boring. Unkind words can tear down a fragile self-image. It is time to deal with such words and their effects in our lives.

When Norman heard me minister about the power of words, he was taken back to a time in his life that he would rather have forgotten completely. Cruel names that had crushed his confidence during his teenage years came flooding back. Hurt feelings that he had pushed down deep inside himself suddenly resurfaced and filled his soul. Norman wept before the Lord. Speaking about the experience afterward, he explained, "I had buried those names so deep inside that I thought I would take them to the grave as a secret. They caused me terrible pain and shame. But as the Spirit showed me that those words were like arrows still lodged in my heart, I allowed Him to heal me. I faced that rejected kid inside, poured out my heart before the Lord, and asked Him to heal me. The peace that I felt when the tears stopped was far greater than the pain that I had carried. For the first time in my life, I can talk and think freely about those times without pain."

TO DO TODAY

Have you been on the receiving end of comments that have hurt your feelings or harmed your self-esteem? Perhaps thoughtless or unkind remarks have dented your confidence, deflated your enthusiasm, or robbed your joy. You may find yourself looking back to your childhood as you think about the words that have injured you. Or perhaps more recent experiences may come to mind. Make a list of any words that have wounded you. It is time to remove every fiery dart from your heart, one by one, and to ask God for His healing.

PRAYER

Father God,

I have been hurt by various words that people have said to me or about me. It damaged me when _____.

[*Be specific about a particular incident: Tell God exactly what was said and how it made you feel.*] Father, I ask You to heal me. By Your grace, I remove every negative and cutting remark from my heart. [*You may need to mention several different experiences. Again, be specific. Picture yourself removing each dart from your heart. In the instances where you know what God's Word says in contrast to those remarks, confess the Lord's love and acceptance over your life in accordance with those Scriptures.*] I ask You to heal my heart completely and to restore my self-image. I ask You to make me whole. I ask You to renew my joy, my dreams, and my confidence. In Jesus' name, amen.

From now on...

We need to know how to immediately deal with negative remarks in the future so that we won't get hurt so easily. The Bible tells us what to do:

[Take] *the shield of faith with which you will be able to quench all the fiery darts of the wicked one.*   (Ephesians 6:16)

To be the best you can be, you need to believe what God says—especially when human opinion contradicts it. If others say, "You can't," boldly declare out loud what God's Word says in contrast to that, such as *"I can do all things through Christ who strengthens me"* (Philippians 4:13). If someone remarks, "You're not good enough," remind yourself of who you are in God, such as is expressed in David's statement *"I am fearfully and wonderfully made"* (Psalm 139:14). We defeat the enemy by putting God's Word in our mouths. Jesus responded to the fiery darts of the devil with the truths of the Scriptures, saying, *"It is written...."* (See, for example, Matthew 4:1–11.) We should do the same. When a "fiery dart" is launched at us, we withstand its power to hurt us by confessing God's Word—and by believing it.

TODAY'S TWEET:

Cutting words wound, but kind words heal.
#detoxforyoursoul

DAY 7

Your Honor

"Lest you give your honor to others."
—Proverbs 5:9

Several years ago, the Lord asked me to minister at a church on the subject of honor. It did not sound like the sort of topic that God would normally speak to me about, so, to be honest, I was a bit reluctant at first. Nevertheless, I cracked on and was blown away by what He showed me. In the Psalms, King David wrote,

> *What is man that You are mindful of him…? For You have made him a little lower than the angels, and You have crowned him with glory and honor. You have made him to have dominion over the works of Your hands; You have put all things under his feet.* (Psalm 8:4–6)

Isn't it amazing to know that the Creator of heaven and earth is interested in the details of our lives? Furthermore, the above passage says that God covers us with glory and honor. The Hebrew word translated as *"honor"* here is *hadar*. This noun comes from a verb that means, among other things, "to glorify" or "to make splendid." It is something that someone does to another person.

When you gave your life to the Lord, He cloaked you with His goodness. He placed a crown on your head and adorned you with beauty.

The Lord knows our vulnerability and our shame, so He covers us with His dignity. He understands the weaknesses of our humanity, so He clothes us with His glory. The Lord does not want to expose our inadequacies. Rather, He seeks to protect us.

Clothed with God's Authority

The above passage goes on to show that when we realize we are robed with God's splendor, we understand our authority in Him. For example, a police officer in uniform knows that he or she carries the full weight of the law. Whenever we see a police officer, most of us stand to attention. We are aware that the officer has legal authority, so we make sure to behave! Similar to the way a governing body grants authority to a police officer, God's honor covers us and equips us. When we are clothed with His glory, we know who we are. We understand our authority in Him, so we can take dominion over the circumstances of our lives. We can be strong.

The Importance of Honoring Others

The following is a well-known mandate from the Old Testament:

Honor your father and your mother, as the LORD your God has commanded you, that your days may be long, and that it may be well with you in the land which the LORD your God is giving you.

(Deuteronomy 5:16)

Most of us know this verse, but its truths are so important that it is worth reviewing. If we want to do well and to have a long life, we need to honor our parents. Unfortunately, the Bible doesn't exclude us from this instruction if we have suffered from a bad upbringing. It is for everyone. If you have experienced rejection, abandonment, or abuse at the hands of those who were supposed to protect you, you might find this commandment particularly hard to swallow. But, I promise you, it is included in the Scriptures for your benefit. When we honor our parents, irrespective of how they have treated us, it brings us great blessing.

Let's look at an illustration of this principle from the life of Noah. After the flood, Noah planted a vineyard and made wine from the grapes.

He might have been celebrating due to his delight at being back on solid ground. Or perhaps he had seen thousands of dead bodies everywhere and had been devastated at the sight. Whatever the reason, he got drunk, stripped himself naked, and fell asleep in a stupor.

Noah's son Ham was the first to find him. He glared at his father and then told his brothers what he had seen. I can imagine him thinking, *Look what Dad has done. What a mess. How pathetic.* (See Genesis 9:20–22.) It can be hard to see those whom we look up to behaving badly. Noah was a good man who messed up. You may have been raised by someone who got it wrong the whole time. If that is the case, ask the Lord to mend your heart. Ask Him to take away the pain of rejection and to pour His healing love into your life.

Noah's other sons, Shem and Japheth, had a very different reaction from that of their brother Ham. They refused to look at their father's nakedness, so they walked backward into his tent, carrying a garment with which to cover him. Noah had gotten horribly drunk and had made a fool of himself. Yet, despite their dad's error, Shem and Japheth reclothed him with honor. They covered his nakedness and restored his dignity. In their hearts, I believe they were saying, *You may have fallen, but you're still our dad. You may have messed up, but that does not make you a mess-up.* (See Genesis 9:23.) The heart of God is the same toward you and me. He intended that we should be treated with respect and dignity, even when we fail. *"While we were still sinners, Christ died for us"* (Romans 5:8). He made provision for our purity while we were in the midst of our mistakes. That's God's heart toward us in both good times and bad.

The Importance of Being Honored by Others

You may have been dishonored by those closest to you. For example, if a dear friend or even the one to whom you were engaged abandoned you, it might have caused you to feel a deep sense of disgrace. We just talked about the fact that parents need to be honored by their children. Therefore, if you are a parent who has been humiliated by your child's rudeness toward you, you might have experienced great shame. Likewise, if you are a pastor or another leader who has been betrayed or belittled by your members or followers, the emotional wounds might run deep. In a marriage relationship, husbands need to receive respect from their wives, and wives need to receive respect from their husbands. Consequently, if you are a husband who has been henpecked or ignored by your wife, such treatment might have robbed you of your sense of dignity. It is equally true that when wives are downtrodden by their husbands, they can feel dreadfully degraded. Perhaps that has been your experience. When a husband or wife is unfaithful, that is the worst wound to bear.

The following Scripture warns men and women to resist sexual temptation.

> *Remove your way far from her* [the *"immoral woman"* (Proverbs 5:3)], *and do not go near the door of her house,* **lest you give your honor to others....**   (Proverbs 5:8–9)

When a married person commits adultery, that person gives the honor that is due to his or her spouse to another. This is one of the reasons why adultery is so painful for the offended party. If you have been hurt by unfaithfulness, it is very important that you ask God to renew you deep down. He desires to restore you and to reclothe you with His honor.

All forms of dishonor rob people of dignity. The people of Nazareth—Jesus' hometown—were offended at Jesus when He taught in their synagogue.

> *So they were offended at Him. But Jesus said to them, "A prophet is not without honor except in his own country and in his own house."*
>   (Matthew 13:57)

Those who had watched Jesus grow up could not handle the fact that one of their own was rising high, so they belittled Him publicly and questioned His value. They showed Him no honor. Interestingly, the phrase *"without honor"* in the above verse comes from a single Greek word, not two words. That single word means "dishonored" or "unhonored." When Jesus was denied the respect that was due to Him, He was being dishonored. In the same way, when you are not given the respect you deserve as a husband, a wife, a parent, a child, a leader, or a friend, you are, in effect, being dishonored.

Reclothed with Honor

Jack's mother was very overbearing. She had her son's life mapped out, and she pushed him in the direction that she thought he should follow. Jack knew that his mother loved him, but he never felt that she trusted him to make his own decisions. As a consequence, his self-respect gradually eroded.

Jack met Emily when he was in his twenties. He quickly proposed, and she accepted. Things started off well, but Emily had a strong, domineering personality. Despite their mutual love for the Lord, Emily struggled to submit to Jack, always wanting her own way. After fifteen years of marriage, Jack felt squashed and stripped of his manhood. Although Emily now understood the importance of submission, the damage had been done. It affected Jack's self-confidence in every area of his life, work, and ministry.

When Jack attended a conference where I shared about the emasculating effects of dishonor, he broke down and wept. The Spirit of God took him back to his childhood, healed him, and then built him up again. He restored dignity to this wonderful man so that Jack could lead his home as God intended.

Several years ago, my husband and I went through a terribly painful experience at church. Accusations were hurled at us, and people drew all sorts of wrong conclusions. I remember telling my husband how it had affected me: "I feel like I have been stripped to my underwear on the platform in front of the people." When the honor that God has given us is taken away, it can leave us feeling ashamed and humiliated. We need to be reclothed by God's glory. If such a situation fits your experience, the Lord wants to restore you today. Your heavenly Father wants to reclothe you with the honor that was stripped from you.

Or perhaps you realize that you need to honor others. Love and honor are different from each other. I can "love" without honoring. We need to both love *and* honor the people whom God has placed in our lives.

Be kindly affectionate to one another with brotherly love, in honor giv-
ing preference to one another.   (Romans 12:10)

When we honor others, we give them special, preferential treatment.
We hold them in high regard and treat them with respect. We seek to cover
their weaknesses, not to expose them. And that's the heart of God for us
and for those around us.

TO DO TODAY

Has anything happened to you that has robbed you of your dignity?
Does the memory of a humiliating or shameful experience make you
squirm? God wants to restore your sense of honor and respect. Face the
difficulty and ask the Lord to heal you.

PRAYER

Heavenly Father,

You have seen the times when I have been dishonored. [*Express
to God what you went through and how it made you feel.*] I ask You to
heal my heart. I receive Your restoring love afresh. Though others
have mistreated me, You always love me. Lord, I see You standing
before me, ready to clothe me with Your honor once again. Where
I have been ashamed, I receive double honor from You. Where I
have been downtrodden, You lift me up. I receive Your crown of
glory. I am reclothed with dignity in Your presence.

Father, I am sorry for the times when I have dishonored others.
[*Name the people whom you have neglected to honor or have actively
dishonored, telling the Lord how you failed to respect them.*] I ask You
to forgive me for denying them the honor that You desired to give
them. Please teach me to show respect to those whom You have
placed in my life. In Jesus' name, I pray. Amen.

TODAY'S TWEET:

My heavenly Father covers me with His honor.
#detoxforyoursoul

DAY 8

Hate's Power

"He who hates, disguises it…."
—Proverbs 26:24

Hate is a strong word. We might assume that we do not hate anyone. However, the Bible says that if we *do* hate someone else, we could be disguising it. Rather than admit to it, we might call it by a different name, saying, "I can't stand her," "She drives me up a wall," or "She's awful." Even though we call it something else, we may actually be harboring hatred toward that person. So, it is probably a good idea to scratch beneath the surface of our lives and check what is in our hearts.

Roots of Hatred

Hatred usually follows hurt. If someone has wounded you, you may feel hostility toward him or her. Even great people can hate others. Consider the example of the brothers of Joseph. Their father, Jacob, loved Joseph more than all his other sons. He allowed Joseph to relax while he sent the other brothers out to work. He did not try to hide his special love for the "dreamer" from the rest of the family. Jacob even bought the "golden boy" a lavish coat and presented it to him in front of everyone.

Joseph's brothers felt deeply rejected by their dad. Most children want to know that their parents love them just as much as they love their other children. When one child is favored, it can be very painful for the others. That's exactly what happened in the case of Joseph's brothers: Their father's favoritism produced deep-seated jealousy, which soon turned to hate. The sons of Jacob, who had been chosen by God to become leaders—patriarchs of the tribes of Israel—detested their sibling! Men like Levi (chosen by God to raise up priests) and Judah (father to a tribe of worship leaders) loathed their own flesh and blood.

> *But when [Joseph's] brothers saw that their father loved him more than all his brothers, they hated him.*   (Genesis 37:4)

If you hate certain people, you usually cannot stand being around them. You struggle to be kind to them, and you want others to share your disdain for them and their behavior. You would like them to suffer the consequences of their bad conduct. If they walk into a room where you are, you probably want to leave. If people sing their praises, you boil inside and might try to set the record straight. Hate may hide its identity, but it never keeps quiet. It whispers words of antagonism, points out faults, and blames and accuses others.

The Devastating Effects of Hatred

Joseph's brothers really hurt him. These promising young men tried to destroy the destiny of the one who had "denied them" the love they deserved. They kicked him into a pit, sold him into slavery, and then told their dad that he was dead. These were not evil men, yet the anger inside them caused them to do some terrible things. That is what hate does.

You might not want to injure your "enemies," but perhaps you want everyone to know their errors. If someone's actions have stolen your happiness or ruined your life, it is no wonder you feel contempt for him or her. However, hate never helps. It is a strong, negative emotion that keeps us bound.

> *He who hates, disguises it with his lips, and lays up deceit within himself; when he speaks kindly, do not believe him, for there are seven abominations in his heart; though his hatred is covered by deceit, his wickedness will be revealed before the assembly.*   (Proverbs 26:24–26)

The above passage shows the devastation that hatred can bring. It opens us up to lying and to cruelty. It seeks to suck us into Satan's evil way of life. God is love, and He brings truth. The devil is hate, and he is the father of lies. (See John 8:44.) When we harbor hostility, we give Satan the right to wreak havoc in us and through us. If we are already wounded, the devil uses hatred to add insult to our injury.

Joseph suffered terrible trials, yet he kept a tender heart toward the brothers who had betrayed him. He endured more than a decade of slavery and imprisonment, but he showed genuine love to the men who had tried to ruin his life. He didn't allow their hatred to infect him. In fact, God used Joseph to bring healing and reassurance to the very ones who had hurt him so badly. (See, for example, Genesis 50:15–21.)

Make the Decision to Reject Hatred

Do not nurse hatred in your heart. (Leviticus 19:17 NLT)

If you recognize even a hint of hatred within you, I encourage you to ask the Holy Spirit to help you to deal with it. We either accommodate our animosity, or we make the decision to kick it out. If we make allowances for ourselves based on the horrendous experiences we have gone through, we will stay in darkness, unable to find a way out. You may wonder why you are struggling to receive answers to prayer, or why you feel like there is a dark cloud over your life. Perhaps it has to do with undealt-with hatred.

He who hates his brother is in darkness. (1 John 2:11)

When we harbor hatred, life feels more difficult. For example, quarrels seem ready to erupt around every corner. It is hard to enjoy ourselves if the object of our anger is anywhere in sight, or even if the person's name happens to come up in conversation. It creates irritation, instead of peace, within us.

Hatred stirs up strife. (Proverbs 10:12)

If you are still affected by the pain you've experienced due to negative past events, it is important for you to ask the Lord to heal your heart. Tell God what happened and how it made you feel. Talk to Him as if you were a child explaining his or her hurt feelings to a loving mother or father. Pour out your heart before the Lord. Then ask Him to heal you.

Once we have dealt with our hurts, it is time for us to let go of our hatred. As we cry out for God's help and lay down all animosity at the cross of Christ, we will start to feel a new sense of freedom. When we choose to give to the Lord all the antagonism that has festered within us, He will take it away. Not only that, but He will also exchange our hatred for His unconditional love. He will replace our animosity with His compassion. He will remove our hardness and give us His tenderness. Those are powerful exchanges!

Inner Restoration

During her childhood, Jane was constantly put down by her older sister, Sophie. Her sister humiliated her at school in front of her friends, laughed at her when she made mistakes, and reported her every error to their parents. By the time Jane left home in her late teens, she was glad to put distance between herself and the sister who had made her childhood so challenging.

After giving her life to the Lord in her twenties, Jane tried again and again to forgive Sophie. Yet, despite her best efforts, Jane always found herself feeling angry when she saw her sister at family gatherings. She could not stand hearing her parents talk about Sophie's achievements, and she always wanted to remind them of her flaws. After years of struggling, Jane attended a meeting where I was ministering about hatred. As the Holy Spirit opened her eyes to what was in her heart, she realized that she had been harboring hatred against her sister for decades. With tears streaming down her cheeks, she asked the Lord to forgive her. She told her heavenly Father about all her hurts and then gave Him the hatred that she had held in her heart. It was like letting go of a heavy burden. Jane asked the Lord to fill her with His love for her sister. The next time Jane saw Sophie, she felt great peace and was able to be kind to her.

Inner restoration helps to keep us free from a whole host of damaging emotions. The more we keep our hearts right, the more we will be well.

Maybe you recognize that you have been harboring hatred. On the other hand, perhaps you suspect that someone who is close to you hates you. You may have made mistakes and afterward asked for forgiveness, but the person still holds you responsible. Or maybe you did nothing wrong, and the root of the hatred toward you is jealousy. Whatever the reason, take on Joseph's traits and keep a tender heart of compassion and forgiveness toward the person. He or she needs your love, not your frustration or anger.

TO DO TODAY

Search your heart to see if there is any hatred within it. Are you holding animosity toward anyone? Have you denied the existence of your hatred, calling it by another name to make it easier for you to handle it? If either of these situations is true for you, make a decision to relinquish your right to your anger, and then lay down every negative attitude. Bring it as an offering to God. Doing so will show just how much you love Him.

PRAYER

Father God,

I have harbored hatred toward [*mention the person's name*], and I want to deal with it today. It hurt me when _____ _____. [*Express to God what happened and how it made you feel. Tell Him about any anger that you have and/or any indignation over injustice that you're holding on to.*] I lay down every ounce of hostility at the cross of Jesus. I ask You to forgive me for holding on to hatred in my heart.

Father, please fill me with Your wonderful love. You are love, and I want more of You in my life. I receive Your love for every person in my past and for those who are present in my life today. Thank You for Your mercy toward me. I will seek to show mercy to others, too. In Jesus' name, amen.

TODAY'S TWEET:

I refuse to harbor hatred & hardness in my heart. #detoxforyoursoul

DAY 9

The F-factor

"Love prospers when a fault is forgiven."
—Proverbs 17:9 (NLT)

Maybe a friend betrayed you, or your spouse cheated on you, or your family abandoned you. Perhaps a colleague took credit for your idea, or an authority figure broke a promise to you. As we discussed yesterday, when someone has wounded us or wronged us, it can be extremely hard to forgive that person and to let it go.

In the year 2000, our first child died before her second birthday. Her name was Naomi, which means "our delight." And that is exactly what she was. A sweet, fun-loving little girl, she had curly blonde hair and bright eyes. She was our angel, and she meant the world to us. However, our precious baby contracted a bacterial infection. Had she been given a simple injection of antibiotics upon her arrival at the hospital, her life would have been saved. If the doctor who had been charged with caring for our little girl had done her job, our daughter would be with us today. Instead, Naomi lay on a hospital bed getting weaker while the medics did nothing. The doctor in charge decided she wanted to wait for a urine sample before treating my sweetheart. As hours passed, I grew more desperate, and I eventually took matters into my own hands. I pressed upon my little girl's tummy, holding an aluminum bowl below it, and I managed to catch a trickle of urine. After the doctor saw this, she conceded and administered antibiotics. But it was too late. The infection had spread through Naomi's tiny frame, causing multiple organ failure. She passed away a few hours later.

Shortly after our daughter's death, my husband and I made a monumental decision. We knelt down before the Lord, with tears running down our cheeks, and forgave the doctor who had been involved in our little girl's death. We asked God to bless her life and her family. We worked with senior practitioners to ensure that new procedures were introduced at the hospital so that no other child would suffer unnecessarily. However, we chose to let go of the wrong committed against *us*. Any time we thought of that doctor, we asked God to be with her and to help her. I believe our heartfelt forgiveness released the healing love of God into our broken lives. Every time I cried out to Him, He tended to my brokenness, and, bit by bit, He put my heart back together. Today, I have no sadness over my daughter's untimely departure. I am deeply grateful that the Lord has restored me and that I will pick up where I left off with Naomi when she and I are reunited in heaven.

Forgiveness Leads to Personal Freedom

No matter what has been done to you, forgiveness is the way to your freedom. When we hold something against anyone, we are inadvertently holding on to that person. Because we won't let go of what the individual did, we can't let go of him or her, either. Unforgiveness keeps us bound to negative events and hurtful people of the past. Yet that is not all. When unforgiveness is left to fester, it can produce resentment and bitterness. Resentment affects our attitudes and our behavior. It can eat us up on the inside.

Resentment destroys the fool. (Job 5:2 NLT)

The Bible says that bitterness can poison us. (See Acts 8:23.) When we do not forgive, we are in danger of poisoning our hearts and choking the life out of our relationship with God. That is why Satan works so hard to coax us to hold on to our hurts. Unforgiveness is the devil's way of making the pain of the past even more potent. However hard it is to let go, doing so is more than worth the struggle.

The heart knows its own bitterness. (Proverbs 14:10)

One of the destructive side effects of unforgiveness is a desire for revenge. If we gloat when those who have wronged us fail, we are living on the wrong side of the fence. Negative emotions can fester. They infect our lives and our relationships. They keep us bound and hardened.

> *Don't say, "I will get even for this wrong." Wait for the* Lord *to handle the matter.* (Proverbs 20:22 NLT)

To forgive, we need to let go of our anger. We must give up our resentment and our quest for revenge, knowing that God alone is the Judge. Although extending forgiveness might be hard for you at first, it will get easier the more often you do it. Whether your anger or hurt involves a colleague at work, a brother or sister at church, or even a spouse or a parent who has deeply wounded you, in the end, the relief that forgiving them will bring will be tremendous. When you get into the habit of letting off those who have harmed you, you will even begin to enjoy forgiving others. It feels good to show mercy, and it is liberating to love. As our key verse says, *"Love prospers when a fault is forgiven."*

Angela was a bright, articulate woman living in Ghana. After thirty-seven years of marriage, she went through a devastating divorce. Her husband had beaten her, cheated on her with a string of women, and withheld money from her. She felt humiliated and heartbroken, and she was on the verge of a breakdown. Soon her agony turned to bitterness and hate. Pastors, friends, and family tried to persuade her to forgive, but she found it impossible to do so. She wanted revenge, and she longed for something terrible to happen to her ex-husband.

Someone gave Angela a CD of my message on forgiveness, and when she heard how God had helped me to forgive the doctor who was on duty when my daughter died, she started to believe that the Holy Spirit could help her, too. Hope began to grow within her. Angela allowed the love of the Lord to flood her heart and to wash away years of anguish and pain. She then made a difficult but determined decision to forgive her husband. She relinquished her right to retaliation and her desire for his demise. It took every effort for her to let go, but she released that man into God's hands. For the first time in years, Angela experienced real peace and genuine joy. Several months later, she bumped into her ex-husband at a family function. Walking toward him, she reached out her hand and greeted him warmly. The look of shock on his face was a picture. Angela was free.

A Lifestyle of Forgiveness

The accounts in the Bible of the softness of David's heart never cease to amaze me. For ten years, King Saul—the man David had once called father—hunted him down, determined to kill him. The young hero lived a rough life, hiding in caves and forests while Saul sent legions of soldiers to execute him. Day in and day out, David lived like a fugitive, fearing for his life. Saul was consumed by jealousy and hatred for the young man, simply because David had won the hearts of the people. On two occasions, David had the chance to kill the king, but he refused to touch the Lord's anointed. (See, for example, 1 Samuel 24:5–10.) Each time the opportunity presented itself, it was at a point when Saul himself sought to murder David. In other words, David had every excuse to retaliate. Yet, not only did David restrain himself, but he also spoke respectfully to Saul when he explained why he had spared the king's life. Then, on the day that King Saul died, David wept and mourned, lamenting that a great and mighty leader had fallen. He said, *"Saul and Jonathan were beloved and pleasant in their lives,…they were stronger than lions. O daughters of Israel, weep over Saul"* (2 Samuel 1:23–24).

What's my point? For ten long years, David lived a life of forgiveness. He let go of anger and apprehension on a daily basis. He kept his heart tender toward a man who had made his life like a living hell, and then spoke of him with love after he died. It is not easy to walk in forgiveness, especially when someone has deeply wounded us. Nonetheless, it is the very best way to live. When we forgive, we can be free from the angst and anger that would otherwise eat us up on the inside. God vindicated David, and, within about a week of Saul's death, the young man was crowned king of Judah. I believe that David's forgiving heart secured his destiny.

The way to tell if you have really forgiven someone is simple. Can you bless that man or woman? Can you talk about him or her with compassion? Do you feel mercy toward him or her? Again, sometimes, the wounds caused by a parent or a leader can hurt the most. These are offenses by someone who was supposed to be caring for you but who let you down, instead. Additionally, rejection in a marriage relationship is one of the hardest wounds to bear. The pain resulting from a partner's disinterest, unfaithfulness, betrayal, or abuse can be excruciating. Nevertheless, forgiving the offending party will clear the way for your heart to be completely healed.

Even if your issue is not so deep-seated, holding on to any type of resentment (no matter how small) is unhealthy. It spoils your relationship with God and hinders your progress. Recently, my husband and I hired a contractor to do some renovations on our home. He asked for 90 percent of the payment up front, completed half the job, and then did nothing for months. I found myself feeling irritated and angry every time I looked at the half-baked job. I had to forgive that man and bless him in prayer in order to protect my heart. Letting go of a grudge brings great relief. Telling someone in your heart, *You don't owe me anything anymore—I'm letting it go,* feels very good. It is like taking back the reins of your life.

Forgiveness is not an option or an extra for those who are on fire for God. It is necessary for anyone who wants a good relationship with the Lord. I depend on God's mercy every time I make a mistake. But I receive pardon from Him only when I, too, forgive:

> *And whenever you stand praying, if you have anything against anyone, forgive him, that your Father in heaven may also forgive you your trespasses. But if you do not forgive, neither will your Father in heaven forgive your trespasses.*   (Mark 11:25–26)

Forgiving others is a no-brainer. We get set free from resentment and bitterness. We get released from the negative events and hurtful people of the past. And we draw closer to God. Do not listen to the devil's lies anymore, so that you remain in unforgiveness. If you do not forgive, the only person who suffers is you. God's way is always the best way.

TO DO TODAY

Assess the state of your relationships. Are you holding anything against anyone? Think about your parents, spouse, siblings, leaders, teachers, managers, colleagues, friends, and so on. If you discover that you have any resentment against other people, make a note of these issues and then pray through each difficult relationship.

PRAYER

Father God,

I realize that I have been holding unforgiveness in my heart. I have been hurt and let down. I have been disappointed and betrayed. [*Name the person who wounded you and tell the Lord exactly what he or she did. Be specific. You may need to go through this exercise several times if you have been harboring a lot of unforgiveness.*]

Today, I forgive [*name*]. I let him/her go. I release all my anger. I relinquish my right to revenge and my entitlement to justice. I am not his/her judge—You alone are the Judge. I choose to show [*name*] mercy, just as You have shown me mercy. I choose to be generous-hearted, just as You are always generous in Your love for Me.

[Continue with this paragraph if the person who offended you is still alive:]

Now, Lord, I ask You to bless [*name*]. I ask You to bless his/her life, family, and work. I ask You to help him/her with any needs.

[Conclude with this paragraph:]

Father, I receive Your sweet presence into my heart again. Thank You for Your amazing grace and for Your wonderful love. I am free! In Jesus' name, amen.

TODAY'S TWEET:

Forgiveness frees me from the hurtful people & pain of the past. #detoxforyoursoul

DAY 10

Confidence

"The LORD will be your confidence."
—Proverbs 3:26

Sylvia lived next door to Mr. Brown, her school headmaster. He was a kind man who believed in her. For the first few years of her education, Sylvia was at the top of her class in every subject. That was until Mr. Brown moved to a different school. With new teachers who dismissed her abilities, Sylvia's grades started to slip. In just one year, she went from being at the top of her class to near the bottom. When someone instilled confidence in her, Sylvia excelled. When people doubted her, she failed.

Growing up surrounded by encouragement, a child has a good chance of becoming confident. Confidence is assurance. It is a form of self-belief. When our daughter Abby was just four years old, a newcomer to the church professed his undying devotion for a soccer team that was the archrival of the one my husband supported. When Abby heard that he supported the "wrong" team, she marched over, sat beside him, and told him that his team was going to lose. The old man jumped to his feet, pointed his finger at her, and retorted, "What did you say?!" Instantly, Abby leapt to her feet, pointed her finger right back at him, and said with a loud voice, "My daddy says your team is rubbish!" It is amazing how much confidence we can have when we know that someone bigger than we are is backing us!

To thrive in the midst of life's ups and downs, and to fulfill our potential, we need confidence. We all encounter various challenges, such as bullying at school, bereavement at home, rejection in romance, poor exam results, ill health, and so on. Support from family and/or friends can help us to regain our strength. But, if such reassurance is inadequate or missing, life's difficulties can strip even a strong soul of a sense of security.

Let's look at two issues related to confidence: (1) a lack of confidence and (2) being "smart and strong."

A Lack of Confidence

One of the most significant prophetic words I ever received was spoken over me at Bible college. I can't remember the topic being taught that day, or why I had gone to the front of the auditorium for prayer. However, I will never forget what the dean of students pronounced as he prayed over me: "You're too small! You're too small in your own eyes." I can still hear those words like it was yesterday.

You are probably familiar with the story of the twelve Israelite spies. Their job was to glean information about Canaan and report back to Moses as the Israelites prepared to enter the Promised Land. God had sworn that He would give the land to His people. He had performed miracle after miracle for the Israelites, delivering them from Pharaoh and then providing for them in the desert. They knew from experience that God was both faithful and able. Yet that was not enough. For God to use them, they had to believe in themselves, as well as in Him. Ten of the twelve spies did not believe that *they* were able. They saw themselves as insects (and, as a result, their enemies looked at them that way, too); in contrast, they saw the competition as giants: *"There we saw the giants…; and we were like grasshoppers in our own sight, and so we were in their sight"* (Numbers 13:33).

You, too, may struggle to believe in yourself. A lack of confidence is usually based on fear. We are afraid that we will be humiliated or ashamed. We are worried that we will be mocked or rejected. We are concerned that we may fall flat on our face. A lack of confidence usually looks inward at inadequacies.

However, remember that the Creator of heaven and earth is *with you*. Not only does He love you, but He also believes in you. He has confidence in you, even when you lack confidence in yourself. Whereas others may have dismissed you out of hand, He gives you His vote. Whereas others may have doubted you, He has faith in you. When you put your trust in Him, He will not allow you to be put to shame. He will protect you. The Lord says,

> I'll be with you. I won't give up on you; I won't leave you.
>
> (Joshua 1:5 MSG)

God designed you and created you. He makes only excellent things, and you are no exception. The Lord wants you to know just how wonderful you are. Remember that King David's father did not believe in him, and his brothers belittled him. (See 1 Samuel 16:10–11; 17:26–28.) However, David had great confidence because he knew deep down that his heavenly Father valued him. David prayed,

> I will praise You, for I am fearfully and wonderfully made; marvelous are Your works, and that my soul knows very well.   (Psalm 139:14)

Trust your heavenly Father's power to turn your life around. Have confidence in His ability to create the circumstances for your light to shine. The Lord is reliable, and He watches out for you. As the above story about my daughter Abby shows, young children feel strong when they are supported by their father. In the same way, you can feel strong knowing that God has your back. He will not leave you.

My love for my children gives them confidence, even though they are now teenagers. They can go to new places or meet new people and be strong in the knowledge that their dad and I are right behind them. We are not necessarily there in person, but we are certainly present in spirit. Our love and acceptance of them helps them to appreciate their uniqueness. And God's love for you and me is so much more affirming. His belief in us can give us cast-iron confidence.

Smart and Strong

Alternatively, you may find yourself at the other end of the spectrum. Perhaps you are a gifted sportsman or sportswoman, or a brilliant businessperson, and your confidence is high. Sometimes, smart people rely on their self-sufficiency. Ironically, when we derive our worth from our talents, it is often because we lacked self-belief before we discovered our strengths. Either way, assurance that is built on achievement is unreliable. Sports stars eventually lose their touch, and business success can come and go. In contrast, if your self-esteem is based on knowing that you are God's masterpiece, it will endure through all the ups and downs of life.

> It is better to trust in the LORD than to put confidence in man. It is better to trust in the LORD than to put confidence in princes.
> (Psalm 118:8–9)

Make sure the value you place on yourself is based on God's view of you. His perception will never change. Put your confidence in Him. The Lord wants us to be confident due to our knowledge that His hand is upon us. When we start to think we are doing well because we are "clever," our confidence shifts from heaven to earth—from that which is certain to that which is fallible. Trust in God's favor rather than relying on your talent.

The psalmist wrote,

> I do not trust in my bow; I do not count on my sword to save me. You [God] are the one who gives us victory.   (Psalm 44:6–7 NLT)

King David was a gifted musician, an outstanding leader, and a superb warrior. However, he never looked to his strengths to make him successful. He depended on God. The Lord wants us to rely on Him in all things. Some of us will probably find that in certain areas of our lives, we are under-confident, but in others, we are too self-sufficient. If that describes you, start to believe that God is able to work through you despite your weaknesses. At the same time, dedicate every gift you have to God, and depend on Him for success. That way, you will look to the Lord more than to anyone or anything else. This will build an unshakeable confidence within you.

> In the reverent and worshipful fear of the Lord there is strong confidence.   (Proverbs 14:26 AMP)

If the Lord says you can do something, believe it. By His grace, you will have the God-given confidence to do it.

TO DO TODAY

Carry out a "confidence audit" of your life, looking at your faith, your family relationships, your home, your ministry, your occupation, and so forth. On a scale of 1 to 10 (10 being highest), rate how much confidence you have in each area. Then ask yourself the following: "What or who gives me my confidence? Is it my talent, or is it knowing who I am in Christ? Or is it a mixture of the two?" Work out where you are in relation to confidence in each area of your life and then pray about your conclusions, placing your full confidence in God.

PRAYER

Father God,

At times, I have doubted myself and felt inadequate. [*If circumstances in life and/or personal experiences have dented your confidence, tell the Lord about them. Explain what was said or done to you and how it made you feel. Pour out your heart, and then ask Him to heal you.*] Today, I put my trust in You. When I am with You, I am protected and secure. I take my eyes off my own shortcomings and look to Your great power.

Where I have put my trust in my talents or my knowledge, I ask You to forgive me. While I will use the gifts and the strengths You have given me, I will not look to them for my confidence. I will choose to rely solely on You, instead. I put my trust in You alone. I look to You for complete security and confidence. In Jesus' name, amen.

TODAY'S TWEET:

God believes in me. #detoxforyoursoul

Step 2

CLEAN OUT

DAY 11

Guilt

"Can a man take fire to his bosom, and his clothes not be burned?"
—Proverbs 6:27

Many years ago, when my husband, Paul, was preaching, he told a story about helping a woman to move from her house. As they sorted through her bags of belongings, he came across a small box. The lady crumpled when she saw the little tin. It contained cannabis from bygone days of backsliding. My husband did not say who the woman was because he knew she still felt ashamed about the discovery. That woman was me. Seeing that tub of dope opened up a cavern of guilt in my soul that I would rather have left alone. It took me back to a time I wanted to forget.

Romans 6:12 says, *"Do not let sin reign…."* God had completely forgiven me years earlier for every mistake I had made. Nonetheless, sin was still reigning over me through guilt. Flashbacks from those dark days made me feel unworthy and unclean. The thought of people finding out about my messes made me cringe.

A lady who had been saved for ten years and been married for twenty wept as she told me that she had not been a virgin on her wedding day. That dear sister had carried guilt in her heart for decades over something that had been dealt with the moment she gave her life to Christ. If any memories (however well hidden) still make you recoil, God wants to set you free. When you are forgiven, that is the end of the matter as far as He is concerned. His will is that nothing from your past can condemn you. That way, Satan and sin lose their power over you.

Knowing this, that our old man was crucified with Him, that the body of sin might be done away with, that we should no longer be slaves of sin.   (Romans 6:6)

The above verse helped to set me free from guilt. I realized that it wasn't just my sin that Jesus had taken to the cross—Jo the sinner had been crucified with Christ. That woman no longer lived. The person who had messed up had been put to death with Jesus. Not only had the sin been done away with but the sinner had been dealt with, too! The new me had been raised with Christ, clean and forgiven. It is exactly the same for you. The new you is blameless before God because of Jesus Christ. Jesus wipes away both the deliberate iniquities and the mistakes of all who are truly sorry. His blood, which is powerful enough to save us, is equally able to cleanse us from every error. His work is perfected in all who ask for forgiveness.

Blameless in God's Sight

Isaiah 53:5 explains that Jesus was wounded and crushed for our transgressions and our iniquities. A "transgression" is when I purposefully go somewhere I should not go or do something I should not do. It is rebellion. An "iniquity" is a warped and perverted deed. Iniquities often lead to patterns of bad behavior. Jesus took the blame and was punished for every one of our mess-ups. In return, He wants you and me to rest in the knowledge that the price has already been paid.

First Corinthians 6:11 (AMP) says,

But you were washed clean (purified by a complete atonement for sin and made free from the guilt of sin), and you were consecrated (set apart, hallowed), and you were justified [pronounced righteous, by trusting] in the name of the Lord Jesus Christ....

Once we have repented, we are washed completely clean. We don't even smell of sin.

It makes no difference what you have done. You might have been in a bad relationship, hurt a loved one with an angry outburst, had an abortion, or spent a lifetime of wrong living. Perhaps you regret the years you have wasted, the opportunities you have missed, or the prayers you have neglected. The Lord died for every mistake you have ever made. Once you say you are sorry and turn aside from wrongdoing, the old passes away, and all things become brand-new. There is no room for shame or guilt. Before God, you are blameless.

You have probably heard the explanation of what justification accomplishes in us. When you trust in the cleansing blood of Jesus to wash you clean, in God's eyes, it is as if you had never sinned. When I am forgiven by Jesus, He looks at me as though I had never messed up in the first place.

If you, GOD, kept records on wrongdoings, who would stand a chance?
(Psalm 130:3 MSG)

None of us would stand a chance if God made us pay for our mistakes. Your faults are no different from mine. I am forgiven today for impatience or pride in the same way that I was forgiven many years ago for impurity. When my children were small and had a row, I would send one upstairs and tell the other to stay downstairs. I separated them. The Bible says that God separates you from your sin *"as far as the east is from the west"* (Psalm 103:12). So, after you ask God to forgive you, He removes your wrongdoing from you. It is no longer yours. It has gone.

If God were a judge in a courthouse, and your case were brought before Him, He would pronounce the decision "Not guilty!" over you. Again, through Jesus, the Lord declares that you are "Not guilty!" Jesus has paid the price for you to live at peace with yourself. He does not want you to carry any condemnation for even one more day.

The chastisement for our peace was upon Him.   (Isaiah 53:5)

"Chastisement" means punishment. Jesus was punished for your faults. He was scourged for your sin. So, why flog yourself? He took the blame so that you could rise up righteous. He does not want you to feel bad about old errors. He wants you to enjoy being righteous in Christ. He longs for you to know the inner peace that an innocent man or woman freely enjoys.

"Comfort, yes, comfort My people!" says your God. "Speak comfort to Jerusalem, and cry out to her, that her warfare is ended, that her iniquity is pardoned; for she has received from the LORD's hand double for all her sins." (Isaiah 40:1–2)

Forgiven and Restored Alike

Jesus not only paid for your forgiveness, but He also made a way for your restoration.

Instead of your shame you shall have double honor, and instead of confusion they shall rejoice in their portion. (Isaiah 61:7)

Jesus does not merely blot out the transgressions of the past; He brightens your future. For every mistake, He gives you a double portion of God's goodness. This is one of the ways that the Lord rubs the devil's nose in his defeat. When we return to the Lord, He blesses us all the more. That is the amazing mercy of God.

The verse above explains just how far God goes to set us free. Again, Jesus not only takes away our guilt, removes all our shame, and cleanses us deep within, but He then gives us double honor. How do we honor people? We respect them, we treat them like VIPs, and we celebrate them. Similarly, the Lord clothes you with honor to show you that a new day has dawned.

TO DO TODAY

Do any of your memories make you cringe with guilt? Do you have any regrets that still cause you to feel embarrassed? Do you feel bad about your shortcomings? Make a list of every source of guilt, shame, or regret that you feel, and then pray over each one. Picture your problems nailed to the cross. The Bible says that God causes *all* things to work together for your good. (See Romans 8:28.) He forgives wrongdoing, removes shame, and turns every situation around. After giving each issue to God in prayer, destroy your "guilt list"—once and for all. Jesus has paid the price. Now it is time for you to walk free, knowing that you are *not guilty.*

PRAYER

Father God,

Thank You that Your mercies are new every morning.

I bring all my guilt and shame before You now. [*Be specific—tell your heavenly Father what you have felt guilty or ashamed about.*] Your Word says that after I repent, You forgive me and take away my wrongdoing. I see my sin—and me the sinner—crucified with Christ. The old [*insert your name*] is dead, and the new me has been raised to life with Jesus. You have separated me from my sin. It is no longer mine. You have cleansed me by the precious blood of Jesus. Because He has already been punished for my trespasses, I will not punish myself anymore. It is over, and I am free. I will not feel bad about these things ever again.

Instead of guilt, You give me a double blessing. Instead of shame, You clothe me with honor and dignity. I am not guilty. I am free. I give You praise and glory. In Jesus' name, amen.

TODAY'S TWEET:

Meet the new me. #detoxforyoursoul

DAY 12

Sex and Stuff

*"Whoever commits adultery…lacks understanding; he…destroys his
own soul. Wounds and dishonor he will get."*
—Proverbs 6:32–33

Sexual sin has a way of causing wounds like no other type of wrongdoing. If I lie, I sin against God. But if I sleep around or look at pornography, I sin against God *and* myself.

*Every sin that a man does is outside the body, but he who commits
sexual immorality sins against his own body.*   (1 Corinthians 6:18)

Sex engages our body and our soul. Our thoughts, our will, and our emotions all get involved. Today's key verses say that when we cross the boundaries God has given us, we literally *destroy* our souls. The word *destroy* means to waste, to spoil, or to injure. While our bodies may not necessarily die as a result of sexual sin, our hearts become deadened.

Sex is meant for marriage. Within a covenantal relationship, it creates intimacy. It brings reassurance and healing, as well as great pleasure. It is an expression of the love and of the lifelong commitment between one man and one woman. When my daughter Abby was about twelve years of age, I was laying claim to my right to a cuddle with her. "Come on, Abby, give me a hug. I think I deserve it. After all, I did carry you for nine months!" Her response was immediate. "But you also had lots of fun rolling around in bed making me!" My husband and I burst out laughing! Sex is fun. It is from God. But it is meant for marriage. In any other context, sex steals and wounds. It soils our purity and damages our relationship with the Lord. It quenches the fire of God in our souls and dulls our spirits. Sex outside of marriage often leaves us feeling ashamed, defiled, and disappointed.

Protect Your Future

With her enticing speech she caused him to yield, with her flattering lips she seduced him. Immediately he went after her, as an ox goes to the slaughter. (Proverbs 7:21–22)

You need to protect your purity for the sake of your future. To do this, you may need to avoid certain people or places. Whether you are married or single, Satan is always trying to trip you up. It is easier to say no right away to a coffee date than to pull back from a kiss. It is easier to do the right thing in the daylight than to resist at night. It is easier to refuse when you are clothed than to be strong when you are naked. We need to create boundaries for ourselves and to live within them.

Attractive people will always be passing by us. Kind colleagues will always be on hand, especially when we are sad or lonely. But a moment's indulgence can cause a lifetime of problems. We need to take captive every wayward thought and to refuse wrong imaginations. (See 2 Corinthians 10:5.) Do not dwell on those dangerous ideas for a moment, thinking that you will purify your heart later on. Be quick to resist every tempting thought and idea.

No one actually *falls* into sin. Sin always starts out as a thought and then, more often than not, becomes a plan. Every imagination that we dwell on grows. Again, we need to kick out every wrong thought. Satan works overtime to try to get us into bed with someone before we tie the knot—and then to keep us out of bed once we are wed.

God Will Renew You

If you have already missed the mark, God will cleanse you. He is the Healer, and He can make you new. When I met the man who would become my husband, I knew he was the one for me. It felt like we had always known each other, and I was at ease around him. Within a matter of weeks, we knew we would be together forever. Although I was excited, I started to worry a little—I would have to tell him about the promiscuity of my past. One afternoon, I plucked up the courage and said, "There's something I need to tell you." His response was immediate: "God has already told me that He has made you brand-new."

"Come now, and let us reason together," says the LORD, *"though your sins are like scarlet, they shall be as white as snow; though they are red like crimson, they shall be as wool."* (Isaiah 1:18)

Though my sins were once like scarlet, God had made them as white as snow. He had cleansed me from the past. The work of the cross was so real that God told my fiancé that He had renewed my youth. I was not soiled goods. I was brand-new.

The same reality renewed Sophie's life. When Sophie was fourteen, she was raped by her mum's boyfriend. Terrified during the attack, she pretended to be asleep; her body froze, and she shut down her mind. Something inside her broke that night, and she spent the rest of her teenage years sleeping around, trying to make sex mean something. When she was nineteen, Sophie started working as a lap dancer in a club, and she regularly sold her body to help pay the bills. She felt this was her lot, and she continued in that lifestyle for four years.

Eventually, Sophie met a man she wanted to marry, and she did her best to settle down in her new married life. Then she had an incredible encounter with the Lord, and her healing began. However, she was still overwhelmed with guilt and shame because of her years of promiscuity. Fourteen years after getting married, and nine years after getting saved, Sophie attended a series of healing meetings that I led. She responded to an altar call and collapsed before God. Every burden of guilt and shame that she had carried was broken, and tears of relief streamed down her cheeks. When she rose from her knees, she knew deep inside that she was completely clean. She felt free for the first time in her life. Now she leads a ministry and sings in her church choir.

Just as God restored Sophie, He can heal you. Too many children in our world suffer abuse, including rape or some other form of molestation, and the effects can be devastating. That is the reason many of us end up living lives that make us feel dirty or defiled. Sometimes, we feel defiled because of what others have done to us. Other times, we feel tainted because of what we have done to ourselves. Either way, God is able and willing to make us completely clean and to renew our youth.

> *And so, dear brothers and sisters, I plead with you to give your bodies to God because of all he has done for you. Let them be a living and holy sacrifice—the kind he will find acceptable. This is truly the way to worship him.*   (Romans 12:1 NLT)

Whatever your story, I encourage you to present yourself to God anew. Young or old, single or married, baggage or no baggage—give your body to the Lord. Give your sexuality to Him. If you need to, ask God to cleanse, heal, and restore you. Then ask Him to help you to change your thinking.

> *Don't copy the behavior and customs of this world, but let God transform you into a new person by changing the way you think. Then you will learn to know God's will for you, which is good and pleasing and perfect.*   (Romans 12:2 NLT)

You may need to ask God to cleanse your thoughts and your imagination. Then dedicate your mind to the Lord afresh and ask Him to set you free from every sin and bondage.

> *Blessed are the pure in heart, for they shall see God.*   (Matthew 5:8)

The blood of Jesus cleanses you from all unrighteousness. (See 1 John 1:9.) Jesus washes your heart, your mind, and your body. He makes you clean and gives you the strength by His Spirit to stay clean.

TO DO TODAY

Think about your body: Do you feel clean? Or do you see yourself as soiled? Do you have complete self-control over your body? Or do you lack that discipline? If you are married, do you have a healthy and happy sex life? If you struggle with any aspect of your sexuality, be open and honest with God today. Tell Him about your worries or difficulties. He is bigger than the things that are bigger than you. In Him, you can overcome these issues and enjoy true freedom.

PRAYER

Father God,

I love You, and I am so grateful for all You have done for me. I come to You today, and I dedicate my body to You. I entrust my sexuality into Your hands.

Where I have sinned, I am truly sorry, and I ask You to forgive me and to cleanse me, Lord. Though my sins were as scarlet, You have made them as white as snow. I turn from my old ways and my old life, and I ask You to give me the strength to live a pure life.

Where I have been hurt, I ask You to heal me. [*Now tell the Lord how you were wounded. Explain how you feel and ask Him to restore you.*] Let Your cleansing blood wash me completely clean of all defilement. You make all things new, and You make me new today.

From now on, I will keep watch over my thoughts, my imagination, and my eyes. I will be careful not to walk into a sexual trap. I rededicate my heart and my body to You. This is a new day, and I rejoice in what You have done and in what You will do in me and for me. In Jesus' name, amen.

TODAY'S TWEET:

I protect my purity for the sake of my future. #detoxforyoursoul

DAY 13

Broken Walls

*"Whoever has no rule over his own spirit is
like a city broken down, without walls."*
—Proverbs 25:28

There was a time when I had little control over my emotions. In fact, I think it would be fair to say that my moods ruled me. When all was well, I was full of smiles and pleasant to be around. However, when disappointments came along or life was tough, I was sullen. If my husband challenged me, I would feel hurt and cry. If a friend misunderstood me, my stomach would tie itself up in a knot. Then there was my time of the month…. I'd be irritable, weepy, and gloomy. It was horrible.

It is not God's plan for you or me to be governed by our moods. If our feelings run our lives, then all it takes is some bad news or a cruel comment from someone to ruin the day. And it is not just women who cave in to their emotions. A male friend who spent some time working in another country explained how he had felt angry all the time he was there. "Everyone drives as though they are in a getaway car: spinning wheels, screeching brakes, and cutting across lanes. I was furious by the time I reached the office every morning. I hated the place!" He allowed his emotions to dictate the tone of every day. As a result, he felt permanently stressed.

The verse above indicates that if we don't rule over our emotions, we are like a broken city without walls. Walls protect a town from an enemy attack. That means that when our emotions are out of control, we are an easy target for Satan. We may snap at our children. (A child spilling a drink and staining the carpet or writing with ink on the walls of our home can rob us of our joy and even spoil our whole week.) Or we may sulk at our spouse for forgetting something we needed. We may get upset with a friend for letting us down. As a result, we don't pray because we are in a huff. We won't go to church because we are too upset (and we use the excuse that it would be hypocritical for us to attend church, when it would actually be helpful). Feelings, feelings, feelings.

Mastering Our Emotions

To live in victory, we need to master our emotions. In fact, Proverbs says we need to *rule* our spirit. There is no doubt that this is easier to do when your heart has been healed. However, just as you can be good with money whether you have little of it or loads of it, so you can be in charge of your feelings whether you are hurting or whole. If you know you need emotional healing, go back to some of the messages from the earlier days in this book and keep pouring out your heart to the Lord regarding your hurts. Read helpful books and attend healing seminars until you really experience restoration. God will lead you on a wonderful journey to wholeness. But, in the meantime, He will show you how to take control.

A fool vents all his feelings, but a wise man holds them back.

(Proverbs 29:11)

"To vent" means "to spring out" or "to release." When we "let it all hang out"—when we allow every negative issue to spill over into our lives—we are falling short of God's best for us. "To hold" means "to constrain," "to calm," or "to quiet." Sometimes, we must hold back our feelings. If we are upset with the way someone has spoken to us, we may need to swallow hard and get over it. There is a time and a place for everything. Years ago, if I was feeling insecure in the middle of the night, I used to wake my husband as he was drifting off to sleep. "Paul," I would whisper in a pathetic whimper, "do you still love me?" Can you imagine it? The guy is just drifting off into sweet sleep, and my insecurity jolts him awake!

Often, we need to calm down. If we are angry or frustrated, we might need to speak peace to the storm inside. If we are irritated at the manner in which someone has spoken to us, we may need to take a deep breath, let it go, and let them off. To give in to every whim is stressful for us, and it saps our strength.

When I was being governed by my feelings, I wanted to be transformed to be more like Christ. However, I did not like it when anyone told me what I needed to change! Eventually, I realized that if I wanted to grow, I would have to accept feedback. This became a training ground for managing my emotions. Instead of showing hurt when people pointed out my shortcomings, I learned to bite my lip and listen. God used my desire to be mature to teach me how to take charge of my soul.

Invest Time and Effort

The soul is made up of three parts—the mind, the will, and the emotions. We need to use our mind and our will to train our emotions. If I know that my feelings are not lining up with God's Word, then I need to assert my will to knock my feelings into shape. For example, if you are discouraged, remind yourself that Philippians 4:4 says, *"Rejoice in the Lord always."* You can praise God despite your distress. And, if you do it from your heart, sooner or later, joy will bubble up inside and strengthen you, and your feelings will change.

The spirits of the prophets are subject to the prophets.
(1 Corinthians 14:32)

Just as the spirit of the prophet is subject to the prophet, so the spirit of the Christian should be subject to the Christian. When we are offended, it is better to say nothing than to say the wrong thing. It is better to count to ten than to lash out. The Bible compares the process of becoming emotionally mature to weaning a child. It normally takes a mother a few months to transition her baby from milk alone to solid food. It requires commitment and a plan. In the same way, learning to manage your feelings will take time and effort, but it will be worth it.

Surely I have calmed and quieted my soul, like a weaned child with his mother; like a weaned child is my soul within me. (Psalm 131:2)

I don't think we will become perfect until we reach heaven, but we can get on the right track. The sense of victory that you will experience every time you react in the right way will sweeten the process.

Something that helped me was my desire to be reliable.

Who may enter your presence on your holy hill?...Those who...keep their promises even when it hurts. (Psalm 15:1, 4 NLT)

Make a decision to be consistent, both when you feel like it *and* when you don't. Do the right thing when you are on the mountaintop *and* when you are in the valley. You will learn to ignore your feelings when they are leading you astray.

If you often struggle with specific emotions, such as sadness or anger, search the Scriptures for verses that you can use to help pull you through. When you are frustrated and want to "let it all hang out," confess God's Word over your life instead. Remember that you won't master your emotions overnight. Nonetheless, if you daily ask for the help of the Holy Spirit, you will get there in the end. As you start to rule your own spirit, you will become a much better and happier you.

TO DO TODAY

Which emotions do you struggle to control the most? On a scale of 1 to 10 (10 being highest), how in charge of those feelings are you? Go through your Bible and find two verses that provide God's answer for each of the negative emotions that try to rule you. For example, if you become depressed easily, the Bible says to *"rejoice in the Lord* **always**.*"* So, make a plan to praise God from your heart every time you are upset. Set a goal for gradual improvement over the next six months. Make notes on your calendar to review your progress at regular intervals. It will take commitment, but you will make it.

PRAYER

Father God,

I have let my emotions have their way. At times, they have dominated my behavior. On occasion, they have suffocated my relationship with You. I am sorry. I ask for Your help to take back control of my own life. I ask You to strengthen me. I will endeavor to do the right thing, whether I feel like it or not. As a mother weans her child, I will train my emotions using Your Word as my guide. I will no longer make excuses for my bad behavior. I will no longer blame others for the way I feel. Instead, I will take responsibility for my actions. When I fall short and allow my emotions to rule over me, I will apologize to You and to others whom I have hurt. Then I will get back up again and continue to train myself. I ask for Your help every day. Thank You for this promise in Your Word: *"Being confident of this very thing, that He who has begun a good work in* [me] *will complete it"* (Philippians 1:6).

Thank You for the wonderful work that You are doing deep within me. I give You praise and glory! In Jesus' name, amen.

TODAY'S TWEET:

I will keep my promises, even when it hurts.
#detoxforyoursoul

DAY 14

Worry

"Anxiety in a man's heart weighs it down."
—Proverbs 12:25 (AMP)

There is so much we can worry about: bills, career, marriage, children, exams, health, and so forth. The list could go on. It is amazing what things will bother us, if we let them. Perhaps anxiety is a normal part of your life—there is always something bothering you, something churning around on the inside. Maybe you are fairly calm until the pressure builds, and then you become overly apprehensive. Your sleep is disrupted, and your mind whirs until circumstances change. Once life is back to normal, you are OK. Or perhaps you usually continue somewhat evenly through life's many ups and downs, but there are niggles at the back of your mind. Either way, the question we need to ask ourselves is whether worry ever helps us.

A Propensity for Worry

Jesus said,

Which of you by worrying can add one cubit to his stature?

(Matthew 6:27)

Some people seem to have a propensity for worry. My daughter Abby was one of them. When she was just six years of age, she came into my room looking all forlorn, and she explained with a quivering lip, "I'm worried, Mummy. I'm worried that I'm not real!" With a glint in his eye and a smile on his face, my husband grabbed a slipper. Pretending that he was going to smack her bottom, he roared, "I'll show you that you're real!" Abby burst into giggles and ran out of the room, screeching at the top of her voice, "I'm real, Mummy, I'm real!"

You can spend a whole night panicking over your problems and re-hearsing every possible outcome of them, but your problems will still be there in the morning. In fact, they will probably seem bigger to you because you will be exhausted. Anxiety is not just unhelpful—it is also harmful.

> *As for what fell among the thorns, these are [the people] who hear, but as they go on their way they are* **choked** *and* **suffocated** *with the anxiet-ies and cares and riches and pleasures of life, and their fruit does not ripen (come to maturity and perfection).* (Luke 8:14 AMP)

Cares can suffocate your faith. When you worry, your mind spins, your heart pounds, and your stomach knots. Perhaps you picture the worst-case scenario. Maybe you become very irritable. At these times, you do not pray to God—you "panic" to Him. Again, it might be that you don't have a full-fledged care but rather a nagging, bothersome thought. But then the worry builds and dominates your thoughts and/or your conversations. Irrespective of *how* worry may affect you or me, it always attempts to choke the Word of God out of us. When we are worrying, we are not believing God. Under these conditions, the problem has usually become bigger in our minds than the Problem-Solver. That is never the answer. The Lord is clear about how He wants us to respond:

> *Do not fret or have any anxiety about anything.* (Philippians 4:6 AMP)

Cast Your Cares on Jesus

There is nothing we face in life that warrants our worry. The currency of heaven is faith. We got saved by faith, we get healed by faith, we receive provision by faith, and we must pray in faith. The way we access God's blessings is by believing His Word. I don't know what struggles you are facing. However, I do know that there is *nothing* too difficult for the Lord.

> *Casting the whole of your care [all your anxieties, all your worries, all your concerns, once and for all] on Him, for He cares for you affectionately and cares about you watchfully.* (1 Peter 5:7 AMP)

If we really understood the Lord's love for us, and His concern for every aspect of our lives, our perspective would change. Not only does He care about every issue that we face, but He also has the power to make a difference. Yet, for us to receive His answers, we need to follow His instructions.

The Lord does not ask us to ignore our angst. He commands us to get rid of it! We cannot muster faith when we are full of fear. Because we access heaven's answers by faith, we need to get rid of every emotion that chokes out faith. We need to deal with anxiety so that we can put our trust in God. The above verse tells us to cast all our concerns onto Him because He cares for us. To "cast" a stone is to throw it away from oneself. God wants us to hurl all our apprehension away from ourselves and onto Him. When we hold on to an issue, it is up to us to sort it out. Yet, when we give it to Jesus, it becomes His problem. He cares about it even more than we do. When He is in charge, all is well.

When I was learning to live without worry, I developed a daily "care-casting" habit. I would quiet myself in God's presence. Then I would name every single issue that was bothering me. One by one, I would tell God why I was worried and then cast each care onto the Lord. I would see myself throwing each problem into God's hands. The load would lighten. Then, as I prayed, it would lift entirely. By the end of my session, I would be relieved and refreshed.

Cathy thought that she had a right to fret. In fact, if she wasn't worrying, she believed that she was neglecting her responsibilities. Angst was a part of her everyday life. Then, when she heard me share about cares, Cathy realized that she had been living life weighed down. She practiced her own daily care-casting sessions. The results were phenomenal. She now enjoys peace and sleeps well. Whenever she is tempted by stress, she stills herself and gives the issue to God.

Come to Me, all you who labor and are heavy-laden and overburdened, and I will cause you to rest. [I will ease and relieve and refresh your souls.] (Matthew 11:28 AMP)

When we go to Jesus with our issues and leave them in His capable hands, He gives us rest. And, when we trust Him instead of worrying, He goes even further: He revives our souls. He pours out His Spirit into our hearts again and renews our vitality.

The Lord does not want us to live with any anxiety. If you have gone from one care to another, God wants you to change your lifestyle. Like Cathy, you probably need to make care-casting a daily habit. Eventually, it will become second nature to you to resist angst. Maybe you do not have a huge problem in this area, but you know that when pressure builds, you become apprehensive. The Lord does not want us to accommodate any concern. Give your cares to Him today and then make a conscious decision to live without worry.

TO DO TODAY

Make an inventory of your responsibilities and an assessment of your current circumstances. As you do this, think about your relationship with each member of your family (one by one) and your close friends. Consider your health, your work, your ministry, your education, your bills, your debts, and so on. Which responsibility/obligation makes you wince or sigh? Is there just one source of your stress or several sources? This exercise will help to show you how many concerns you are carrying. Now it is time to lay each one down in prayer. Don't try to lump everything together as you pray. You need to give each issue to God, one by one. That way, you will know that you have truly let go of every angst.

PRAYER

Father God,

I have been worried. Today, I come to You with my burdens and my anxieties. [*As you pray, name every apprehension. Use your inventory/assessment as a checklist in prayer. Be specific and see yourself bringing every load to Him, one by one. Tell Him why you have worried and how you have felt. Picture yourself laying down each care in His presence.*] I bring every worry to You. I give You every fear and angst. I cast all my cares onto You because You care about me. I lay down every concern, and I leave them all with You—once and for all.

I thank You that every answer to every problem is in You. I will no longer try to fix these problems myself. You are my loving heavenly Father. I trust You. I know that You are more than able to see me through every situation. I place my life in Your hands. I leave every burden with You.

Now, in exchange for my burdens, I receive your refreshment. I enjoy the rest that comes from having faith in You. I thank You for Your love and for Your wonderful presence. In Jesus' name, amen.

TODAY'S TWEET:

Worry? It's God's problem! #detoxforyoursoul

DAY 15

Offense

"A brother offended is harder to win than a strong city."
—Proverbs 18:19

Someone takes your place in line, your pastor walks by without saying hello to you, your friend leaves you stranded without a ride, or you give your best and no one notices. Life is full of opportunities to be offended. Offense is a sense of umbrage, outrage, or hurt. When we are offended, we say things like "It's not fair," "How could she?" and "That's not right!"

An offense usually starts small, with a whisper or a thought.

Now a word was secretly brought to me, and my ear received a whisper of it. In disquieting thoughts…. (Job 4:12–13)

The thought is not the offense—the offense is our negative response to the thought. By rehearsing the incident, the whisper starts to disturb us. We recount what we wish we had said or what we think another person should have done. Indignation builds within us.

Four Sources of Offenses

An offense normally comes from one of four sources. (1) It can be caused by what people say, such as an unkind comment or a rude remark. (2) It can be prompted by what people do *not* say. For example, offense can come when no one thanks you for your hard work, or when your spouse fails to notice your new hairstyle or a purchase you have made. (3) It can be provoked by what people do. Perhaps someone takes your usual seat in church while you are standing nearby talking to a friend, or a fellow shopper pushes you out of the way so he or she can grab the last copy of a book you wanted. (4) It can be set off by what people do *not* do. Maybe no one calls to see how you are doing when you are sick, or the pastor does not visit when he said he would, or your family forgets your birthday.

My friend Ellie went to a café, ordered a coffee and a chocolate bar, and found a seat. A lady sat down opposite her and, to Ellie's horror, the woman started eating the chocolate. As soon as the lady put the half-eaten bar down, Ellie grabbed it, stuffed it in her mouth, and shouted, "There you go!" Still furious, Ellie stormed out of the café, simmering about the rudeness of that woman. Reaching into her purse for her car keys, she saw *her* chocolate bar! The lady was completely innocent, while *she* was the guilty one.

As Jesus explained the parable of the sower to His disciples, He said,

> *The ones sown upon stony ground are those who...have **no real root** in themselves, and so they endure for a little while; then when trouble or persecution arises on account of the Word, they immediately are **offended** (become displeased, indignant, resentful) and they **stumble and fall away**.* (Mark 4:16–17 AMP)

Offense is serious. It steals the Word from our hearts, making us stumble and fall away. People have forsaken friends, left churches, quit jobs, and resigned from positions, all because they were offended. Offense is a test that every one of us has to pass again and again if we are to fulfill our destiny. Many times, we might claim that we are just "cross" or "upset," but, in truth, we are probably offended. And, as today's key verse says, when this happens, it is very hard for anyone else to bring us around: "A brother offended is harder to win than a strong city."

The Answer to Offense

If a brother or a sister is going to have to struggle to bring me back from the brink of offense, as this Scripture indicates, it would be best for me to learn to spot offenses in my own life and to quickly expel them. Offense breeds pride (that sense of superiority and judgment over others), and pride breeds offense. When we feel wronged, we all too easily harden our hearts. Others may try to offer correction, but we think they have no right to do so. In other words, we batten down the hatches and push people away.

You and I are the answer to offense! We have to watch our own hearts like a hawk. We must learn to humble ourselves and to accept the truth. We have to acknowledge that we will probably get offended from time to time, and we need to be ready to spot our faults. Addressing an offense is a wonderful opportunity to kick pride out of our lives.

Part of the process of maturing in Christ is to learn to love others when our flesh wants to react negatively against them. Jesus told us in the parable of the sower that we will be easily offended if we have no real root in ourselves. What is the root that Jesus was speaking about? It is love. In Paul's letter to the Ephesians, the apostle prayed that God's people would be *"rooted and grounded in love"* (Ephesians 3:17).

Love is patient when people are unpleasant. It is kind to the callous and uncaring. If someone makes a mistake, love believes the best about the person. It is not easily provoked, even by arrogant or rude behavior. Love never insists on its own rights but thinks of others first. Love covers. (See 1 Corinthians 13:4–7.) If my heart is filled with this kind of love, then it will be very difficult for me to get offended. Love is the antidote to offense.

Pursue peace with all people, and holiness, without which no one will see the Lord.   (Hebrews 12:14)

We are instructed to pursue peace with *all* people. That includes a demanding in-law, a malicious manager, a difficult leader, and even an awkward usher. What situations press your buttons? Who makes you shake your head in annoyance or causes your blood to boil? The Lord commands us to pursue peace with those people, too. The word *"pursue"* in the above verse means "to run after or eagerly seek." We have to put our hearts into living in harmony with everyone.

Brad went on holiday with his extended family to celebrate his mother-in-law's seventieth birthday. All was going wonderfully well until his brother George showed up. The two brothers had often argued at home, so, before George had even arrived, Brad was wary. However, nothing could have prepared him for the week ahead. George's two young girls were unbelievably naughty the entire time. They tore around the house like wild animals, knocked over tables in their grandmother's sitting room, and generally caused havoc. The youngest went hurtling around the garden with snot on the end of a stick, yelling, "The bogeyman is coming to get you!" When Brad suggested to George that he should control the children, his brother became aggressive. The atmosphere in the house turned very tense. Brad could barely look his brother in the eye. But he had brought with him a copy of my teaching on offense, and he started to meditate on it. Every time anger arose within him, he chose to let go and to love, instead. He went on a kindness offensive, and, little by little, he created a sanctuary of peace for himself. The enemy wanted to provoke him to start a conflict and ruin the holiday, but Brad chose a better way. Love won.

When our little daughter died, we drove back from the hospital in a daze. We were traveling in the fast lane but at a snail's pace. The driver behind us became very annoyed, beeping and flashing his lights at us. Slowly, we moved out of his way. This experience taught me an important lesson. You never know what someone else is going through. Sometimes, the way people are behaving has nothing to do with you, and everything to do with their own difficult journey. I try to remember that. If someone hurts your feelings, mistreats you, or gets in your way, why not make a decision to be gracious and kind? For example, if a neighbor does something that bothers you, overlook it for love's sake and be kind to him or her in return. It is amazing how much more enjoyable life is when we overlook the mistakes people make and give folk the benefit of the doubt. Imitate God, who said, "I will remember your sins no more." (See, for example, Jeremiah 31:34.) Let the offense go, and put on love.

> *The discretion of a man makes him slow to anger, and his glory is to overlook a transgression.* (Proverbs 19:11)

We need to make every effort to keep our hearts free from frustration. People who are easily offended easily offend others. Even those who don't normally get offended can be angered by those who are often offended. You

96 30-Day Detox for Your Soul

probably know someone who gripes and grumbles at nearly everything. Be careful to show extra kindness to that individual. If you come across a brother or a sister who is always agitated, practice patience. Paul said,

> *I myself always strive to have a conscience without offense toward God and men.* (Acts 24:16)

Let us remove all indignation and upset from our lives and keep our hearts clean. Join Paul and aim to live free from all offense. Please don't kid yourself that doing so is easy, but make every effort.

TO DO TODAY

Is there anyone in the various spheres of your life who has made you angry or upset? Make a decision to be totally honest in your heart as you consider this question. Instead of using labels or euphemisms to cover your umbrage, admit it to yourself when you have been offended. That is the first step in dealing with offense. Then pray about the offenses you have held on to.

PRAYER

Father God,

I thank You that You forgive and forget my sins. I realize that I have held offenses against others. Please forgive me. [*If there are people with whom you are upset or angry, tell the Lord. Explain how they have offended you, and give their transgressions to God. Tell Him that you let them go. Forgive and forget.*] I let go of every offense in my heart. Love believes the best of other people and is patient toward them. I choose to show love instead of indignation. I will be patient and kind, even when it is difficult. I let go of my right to justice. Help to keep me free from all offenses, I pray. In Jesus' name, amen.

TODAY'S TWEET:

For love's sake, I will overlook the wrongs of others. #detoxforyoursoul

DAY 16

What Do People Think?

"Many seek the ruler's favor,
but justice for man comes from the LORD."
—Proverbs 29:26

One day, when my daughter was eight, she came home from school upset. "I wish you and Daddy had proper jobs! My friends' parents do normal things. They're teachers, chefs, and journalists. It's embarrassing telling people that you are pastors. Mummy, please go back to an ordinary job!" She was afraid that her friends would tease her or look down on her. Fear can be crippling. For many years, I was preoccupied with the opinions of other people. I would worry about what I had said. For example, I would be anxious if I thought I had said too much or too little. I would be concerned if I thought I had been too loud or even too quiet (although the latter was a rarity, I promise you!). If I thought I had upset someone or given the wrong impression, I would lie awake at night, turning the situation over in my mind.

People-Pleasing

Today's key Scripture says, *"Many seek the ruler's favor." Many* means large numbers of the population. It is a word that is used to refer to multitudes. In short, it means most people. So, the implication is that the majority of us struggle in some way with people-pleasing.

"To *seek*" is to crave after or long for. Seeking the ruler's favor means trying to win the approval of those who are important. We can apply the word *"ruler"* to a dominant person in our lives. It might be a boss, a partner, a spouse, a special friend, a parent, or even a leader. It is the person whose opinion means everything to us. When that person is happy, all is well with us. However, when he or she disapproves of what we are doing or saying, we become distressed. We will do whatever it takes to regain favor with him or her, even if it means changing our plans or our opinions.

The word *"favor"* literally means "face." This corresponds to how we look to see the person's reactions, and we long for an encouraging smile or an approving nod. When we secure his or her support, all is well with us again. That is called people-pleasing—and it is a trap.

> *Fearing people is a dangerous trap, but trusting the LORD means safety.*   (Proverbs 29:25 NLT)

When we are people-pleasers, receiving a stern glance from a person across the room or being presented with a challenging question from someone can make us squirm and cave in. The thought that we might have offended someone important can fill us with dread. Again, we may end up doing whatever is necessary to try to win back the person's approval. Fear saps our inner strength, making it easy for the enemy to control us. We should not be *scared* of upsetting anyone. As Christians, we want to honor others, but we should never allow fears about their possible reactions to determine our thoughts or our decisions.

> *You shall not be afraid in any man's presence.*   (Deuteronomy 1:17)

Martina became increasingly self-conscious as a teenager. She would shrivel up inside if teachers put her down. As the years went by, she grew afraid of all authority figures. By the time she had reached adult life, she had become a very timid lady. Martina ran from any prospect of recognition or responsibility and tried to hide in the shadows. She didn't like meeting new people, especially if they were important. That was just the way she was, or so she thought.

When Martina attended a series of meetings I held on the topic of fear, she felt as though a mirror was being held in front of her face. She had pigeonholed herself as shy, but now she knew that she had been crippled by fear. She realized that if she was going to fulfill God's plans for her life, she would have to deal with this giant. Martina made a monumental decision, declaring, "From this day, I will obey God, not fear. I will seek His approval, not man's!" She continued fighting fear until it lost its controlling power over her. Today, Martina is a phenomenal worship leader at a major city church.

The Bible constantly cautions us not to fear. In fact, Scripture tells us to not be afraid on 365 different occasions. That is one reminder for every day of the year! For most of us, overcoming fear is a journey. Maybe you have lived your whole life worrying about what people think of you, and you want to be free. Or perhaps you have had some victories over people-pleasing, yet you still sometimes hanker after approval or admiration. It is important to locate your position on the "fear spectrum." When we acknowledge the truth, we can be set free.

The LORD is my Light and my Salvation—whom shall I fear or dread? The Lord is the Refuge and Stronghold of my life—of whom shall I be afraid? (Psalm 27:1 AMP)

Breaking the Power of Fear

You are a child of the Most High. He is your Protector, your Provider, and your Promoter. His opinion is the only one that really matters. He is the only One you really need to please. Intimidation is crushing, and it is not your portion.

For God has not given us a spirit of fear and timidity, but of power, love, and self-discipline. (2 Timothy 1:7 NLT)

If we want to fulfill our potential, we will have to break fear's controlling power. If we give in to fear, we will always struggle to obey God. It takes courage to conquer our fear. However, it is more than worth it in the end. Fear is an enemy of God, and it is an enemy of ours, too.

Do not be afraid; only believe. (Mark 5:36)

Again, before we can walk in faith and victory, we need to deal with our fear. We cannot just ignore it or pretend it does not affect us. We must stop it in its tracks. Here are three steps to doing this.

Step one: We need to repent, because fear is sin. It is the opposite of faith. When we are afraid, we are not trusting God. When we cave in because we fear other people's opinions of us, we are taking our eyes off the Lord and looking to others for answers. We are trying to please people instead of seeking to please God. So, we need to tell the Lord we're sorry and ask Him to forgive us.

Step two: We need to rebuke the spirit of fear. The Bible clearly says that fear is not just a feeling or a thought, although that's how it enters. Fear is a demon that tries to torment God's people. That should not worry you. The devil pretends to be a lion. In reality, he is just a snake!

Your adversary the devil walks about **like** *a roaring lion.*   (1 Peter 5:8)

When we submit to God and resist the devil, the enemy scatters. We resist him by commanding him to leave our lives in the name of Jesus. He cannot withstand the name of Jesus. Fear cannot handle our authority in Christ.

Submit to God. Resist the devil and he **will** *flee from you.* (James 4:7)

Step three: We must change our thinking. Our life is in God's hands. He is our Provider, our Protector, and the One who will raise us up. Justice, healing, and prosperity come from Him. Turn your attention from human beings to your Maker. When you feel like looking across the room to see if that key person approves of you, stop. Instead, look up and ask God for His support. Say to yourself, *It does not matter what people think. It matters what God thinks.* He is faithful.

And He who sent Me is with Me. The Father has not left Me alone,
for I always do those things that please Him.   (John 8:29)

Delight in the Lord's approval from now on. Start each day determined to honor and obey Him. Remind yourself regularly, "I live to please God." If there are times when you normally would have sought the opinions and reactions of others, make a decision not to ask and not to try to determine what they are thinking. When we are totally free from the opinions of other people, we can enjoy life so much more. And we can start to fulfill our true potential and our God-given destiny.

TO DO TODAY

Review your relationships with your family members, coworkers, leaders, and so forth. Is there anyone whom you try to impress? Is there anyone who intimidates you? Is there someone who makes you shrivel up inside? If so, write down the names of those who affect you in these ways, and pray over them. Bring every imbalanced relationship to the Lord. From now on, renew your mind anytime you think man-pleasing thoughts. Resist every temptation to fear. Continue fighting until the battle is won.

PRAYER

Father God,

For far too long, I have worried about what others think of me. I realize that I have been preoccupied with pleasing people. [*Mention those individuals whose names you wrote down.*] I am sorry, Lord, and I ask You to forgive me. I now renounce the fear of man. I will no longer live my life in its grip. I rebuke fear, and I take authority over every intimidating spirit. I will no longer do what fear prompts me to do. Instead, I will do what God says! Lord, You are my All in All. You are my Provider, You are my Protector, and You are the One who will raise me up. I put my trust and confidence in You alone. In Jesus' name, amen.

TODAY'S TWEET:

It doesn't matter what people say about me, because I know what God thinks of me. #detoxforyoursoul

DAY 17

Thoughts

"As [a person] thinks in his heart so is he."
—Proverbs 23:7

What I think about myself determines the person I become. I must therefore be more convinced by my own opinions than by those of others. Other people's views will have an impact, but my inner beliefs about myself map out my future. They draw a boundary around my potential. If I think I am capable, I will achieve much more than if I doubt my competence.

Psychologists studying the effects of positive thinking took one hundred people at random and divided them into two groups. Those in group one were encouraged to believe that they would complete a sporting task very quickly. In contrast, those in group two were told that they would struggle. Guess what? The members of the group who thought positively completed their task significantly more quickly, even though there was no difference in ability between the two teams. What we think not only affects our outlook but also has an impact on our performance in life.

But those things which proceed out of the mouth come from the heart.
(Matthew 15:18)

Heart Meditations

The devil works overtime to limit our progress by sowing negative ideas in our minds, such as the following: "You can't stand on the platform with the other leaders; you're not mature enough." "You don't deserve a promotion; you're not smart enough." "You will never break that habit; you don't have the willpower." "That won't work." "You aren't good enough." What you meditate on in your heart will shape your attitude, and it will eventually find its way out of your mouth through your declarations about yourself. And when you say it, you will be even more likely to believe it.

We need to pay particular attention to thoughts that are *close* to the truth but are untrue. For example, if you struggle to get up in the morning to pray, you may wrestle with the thought that you'll never change. James 1:15 says that desire gives birth; so, if you truly hunger for a great prayer life, you will get there in the end. For years, I struggled to establish a daily devotional time. Nonetheless, I eventually achieved it. When I stopped doubting myself and instead believed that God had given me the self-discipline I needed, things started to turn around.

If you struggle in that area, quote God's Word—such as *"Early will I seek You"* (Psalm 63:1)—believe that you will get there, and keep persevering. If you struggle in the area of purity, you will probably need to deal with the feeling that you will never win the battle. Empty yourself of all negativity, remember that God is bigger than the things that are bigger than you, and be determined. You can conquer. Many have gone before you and are cheering you on.

Unfortunately, when we entertain pessimism, we open the door to self-pity. That drags us down further and keeps us in defeat. "I'll never get a new job" (negative self-talk) leads to "It's not fair; nothing ever works out for me" (self-pity). When we feel sorry for ourselves, we usually pamper and nurture wrong thinking. However, such a mind-set needs correction, not sympathy. Self-pity will always hinder our success. We need to see gloomy attitudes as enemies of God's purposes and take them captive.

> *Casting down arguments and every high thing that exalts itself against the knowledge of God, **bringing every thought into captivity** to the obedience of Christ, and being ready to punish all disobedience....*
> (2 Corinthians 10:5–6)

When you notice yourself doubting your ability, stop it. Say out loud, "I'm not putting up with bad thinking anymore!" Instead, declare, *"I can do all things through Christ who strengthens me*" (Philippians 4:13). Even if you have to speak quietly under your breath, use your words to straighten your thinking. When you hear yourself questioning your commitment to change your outlook, grab that thought and put it out of your mind. Replace that view with heaven's perspective: "I am made in the image of the Greatest!" Our job is to reject ideas that do not line up with God's Word. We must refuse hopelessness and instead believe that God is able. The Word says,

> *Whatever is not from faith is sin.* (Romans 14:23)

Let Your Thoughts Work for You

We need to view negativity, condemnation, and unbelief as sin. Let your thoughts work *for* you and not *against* you. Do not tolerate inner conversations about your inadequacies or failures. If you have made a mistake, then repent. Enjoy the Lord's love and forgiveness. If you have tripped up, then get up, dust yourself off, and take hold of God's promises again. Do not rehearse your wrongs. Concentrate on God's compassion. Don't look back. Rather, fix your face like flint on fulfilling your purpose. (See, for example, Isaiah 50:7.) I spent a day counseling a sweet lady with a kind heart who had convinced herself that she was the "whore of Babylon"! (See, for example, Revelation 17.) This dear sister had allowed herself to become obsessed with nonsense because her thoughts ran wild.

> *Don't copy the behavior and customs of this world, but let God transform you into a new person by changing the way you think.*
> (Romans 12:2 NLT)

If you want God to transform your life, you need to change your mind. The devil tries to tell us that we are powerless, that our negative thoughts are just part of our personality. That is simply not true. We have control over our thoughts, so why don't you start putting God's Word—instead of doubt—in your heart?

At the time when I rededicated my life to the Lord, a whole host of negative thoughts used to run riot in my imagination. I dwelled on past mistakes, and I thought I was unreliable, so I could not imagine myself succeeding. But then I took Philippians 4:8 (ESV) to heart: *"Finally, brothers, whatever is true, whatever is honorable, whatever is just, whatever is pure, whatever is lovely, whatever is commendable, if there is any excellence, if there is anything worthy of praise, think about these things."* I replaced wrong thoughts with lovely thoughts. Every time I found myself in negativity, I deliberately moved into positivity. At first, my actions felt forced. Within a matter of weeks, however, I was a more positive, faith-filled person.

> [The Lord said,] *I will put My laws in their mind and write them on their hearts.*   (Hebrews 8:10)

Picture your heart like a clean whiteboard. Now imagine all the negative words that you have written on that space (for example, words of condemnation, inadequacy, and despair). All too often, we then try to write God's Word directly on top of those negative words. But that creates an illegible mess!

> [Jesus] *takes away the first* [covenant] *that He may establish the second.*   (Hebrews 10:9)

We need to tell the Lord about any negative views of ourselves that we have held, and ask Him to wipe them away at their very root. We need to bring recurring wrong thinking to the Lord, acknowledge that it is out of line, and ask Him to take it away. When pessimism is removed, we can start to write God's Word on the blank canvas of our cleansed heart.

TO DO TODAY

Do you have any negative thought patterns? Maybe you have believed certain erroneous ideas for quite some time. Do you question your ability, your purity, your attitudes, or your value? Have you believed that nothing will ever change, that you are stuck, that there is no way out? Tell the Lord what you have believed, and why. Then ask Him to forgive you and to uproot all negativity. After that, search the Scriptures for what God says about the very issue(s) you have dealt with. Find two or three verses that speak to your spirit, and allow God's Word concerning those matters to sink in. For example, if you struggle to believe in yourself, meditate on

Philippians 4:13: *"I can do all things through Christ who strengthens me."* Think about what the Bible says and choose to believe Scripture instead of Satan's lies. Confess those verses over your life on a daily basis. If any old thoughts try to creep in, throw them out and remind yourself of what the Bible says. That's the truth!

PRAYER

Father God,

I realize that I have entertained doubts and pessimism. I have dwelled on my problems and inadequacies. I bring all that negativity to You. [*Now tell God what you used to think, and why.*] I ask You to forgive me because anything that is not of faith is sin. I am sorry that I doubted Your power to do amazing things in me and through me. Your Word says that I will be transformed when I change the way I think, so I ask for Your help to renew my mind. From now on, I will endeavor to take captive every negative thought to the obedience of Christ. I will put Your Word in my heart and in my mouth. I will believe Your promises and speak them over my life. In Jesus' name, amen.

TODAY'S TWEET:

I believe that God is able. #detoxforyoursoul

DAY 18

Motives

*"People may be pure in their own eyes,
but the LORD examines their motives."*
—Proverbs 16:2 (NLT)

When I became a Christian as a teenager, I was hungry to grow spiritually. I never missed church, praised God with all my heart, and listened intently to any preacher. Week after week, I accompanied friends to the altar as they responded to salvation calls. Leaders encouraged me, delighted by my passion. I loved my new life. Although I went through some serious ups and downs in my Christian walk, I never doubted the call of God on my life. In my twenties, I attended Bible school, got married, and joined my husband in ministry. I soon discovered that I loved to preach. I sought the Lord for His Word, pressed in for greater revelation, and ministered to the people. I was delighted with the response as many received from His Spirit.

One day, as I was praying, God spoke to me through the life of Hezekiah, one of Israel's greatest leaders. King Hezekiah loved the Lord wholeheartedly and did what was right in His sight. At the same time— like so many of us—he had an Achilles' heel. Near the end of his reign, he heard that messengers from the powerful Babylonian royal family would be visiting his kingdom. I imagine he was very excited about the visit. "To think that representatives of important world leaders are coming to see me!" he might have exclaimed.

I believe Hezekiah was starstruck and became determined to impress them. In his attempts to look good, he said things he should not have said and showed them things he should not have revealed. Hezekiah served God with all his heart, but, at the same time, he loved the praises of influential people (a topic we began to address on Day 16 of our journey, "What Do People Think?"). On one hand, he wanted to please God. On the other, he enjoyed applause. (See 2 Kings 20:12–18.) And, in my prayer time, the Lord put the mirror of His Word in front of my face and said, "That's you."

I had always loved God. However, for as long as I could remember, I had always craved attention, as well. Whether it was work or ministry, comments such as "Great job," "Fantastic message," or "Well done" gave me a real buzz. I fed on positive feedback. Although I recognized the truth when the Lord showed it to me, I had not been conscious of it before. I made a decision to no longer listen to applause, and I weaned myself off people's praises. While still appreciating people's responses, I would not allow myself to "drink in" compliments or congratulations. As I broke the habit, I often felt empty after ministering. God then redirected my heart so that I learned to seek His affirmation and not that of other people.

Hidden Intentions

Every way of a man is right in his own eyes, but the LORD *weighs the hearts.* (Proverbs 21:2)

It is all too easy to focus on the major things and to ignore the minor ones. I could have reassured myself that I sincerely loved the Lord and that my goal was to please God (the major). However, to mature and to become more useful, I had to face the truth that I enjoyed people's praises (the minor). It takes only a speck of excrement to defile a gallon of pure spring water. If we want to enjoy more of God's presence and power, we will have to focus on some minors so that we can become pure.

There are many traps we can fall into. Name-dropping is sometimes a problem in the body of Christ. We deliberately mention the names of important people we have met or the great places we have visited because we think it will impress others. Sometimes, we do good things for the wrong reasons. Perhaps we give money when the offering bucket is passed because we want to appear generous. Maybe we help out in the nursery at church because we want the folk there to like us. Perhaps we seek a certain position because we want to be respected. With God, motives mean everything.

> *Fire tests the purity of silver and gold, but the LORD tests the heart.*
> (Proverbs 17:3 NLT)

We need to ask the Lord to search our heart and to reveal our hidden motives. Very often, we don't even realize that our intentions are wrong until the Lord shows us the contents of our heart. We can join David, a man after God's own heart, in prayer:

> *Put me on trial, LORD, and cross-examine me. Test my motives and my heart.*
> (Psalm 26:2 NLT)

When you fast, do you like people to know about it? If you have done something kind, do you tell others? When you serve, do you want to be noticed? Do you speak about your talents or experiences in order to impress your peers? Do you prophesy or pray aloud so that folk will know that you are "spiritual"? Do you want to be a leader partly because of the privileges and the position? Everything we do should be propelled by our love for God and our love for other people.

> *The LORD's light penetrates the human spirit, exposing every hidden motive.*
> (Proverbs 20:27 NLT)

Becoming Pure in Heart

It is tempting to deny our shortcomings and to carry on as we are. It is easy to make excuses. But when we humble ourselves and acknowledge our errors, the Lord can work with us.

> *Don't excuse yourself by saying, "Look, we didn't know." For God understands all hearts, and he sees you. He who guards your soul knows you knew.*
> (Proverbs 24:12 NLT)

We find out what drives us when all external rewards and recognition are removed. When God alone is pleased, how do you feel? When there are no human thanks for your efforts, no pats on the back, no admiring looks or smiling faces, how do you respond? When there is no chance of promotion or position, do you serve as steadfastly?

Awareness is the beginning of change. Once we know what is wrong, we can start to do what is right. If you are aware that you like people to know when you are fasting, don't tell anyone. If you pray aloud or quote from the Bible to look spiritual, keep your mouth shut in meetings. If you talk about your talents too much, then start celebrating other people's successes, instead. Starve yourself of the very "reward" that used to motivate you.

Often, these issues are rooted in pride—the desire for human recognition rather than (or more than) the Lord's. God resists the proud. By contrast, He shows great favor to the humble. (See, for example, James 4:6.) Ask the Lord to expose any pride within you. Although the disclosure will be unpleasant at the time, the freedom that will follow your repentance will be phenomenal. When we allow the Holy Spirit to expose the negative motivations that drive us, and to purify our hearts, we prepare ourselves for abundant blessing.

> *He who loves purity of heart and has grace on his lips, the king will be his friend.*   (Proverbs 22:11)

The more you cleanse your motives, the closer the King will come. You will notice new life in your relationship with Christ.

TO DO TODAY

If you recognize that certain rewards other than pleasing the Lord motivate you, make a note of them. It might be the buzz you get from telling people who you know or what you do. Perhaps you like to tell friends when you are fasting or praying, or how well you know the Bible. Ask the Holy Spirit to show you what is in your heart. Now decide to starve yourself of those benefits. That may mean shutting the ears of your heart to people's words. Be gracious as they congratulate you, but do not let their words feed you. It could be that you will need to stop talking about your achievements.

It may be that you will need to stop seeking to build relationships with people who could help you to climb the "ladder of success." The Holy Spirit will show you how to cut off wrong rewards. Doing so will purify your heart.

PRAYER

Father God,

I want to do everything out of a pure heart. I ask You to examine me. Show me the motivations that drive me—whether they are positive or negative. Where my motives have been wrong, I ask You to forgive me. Where I have looked for human recognition, position, or privilege, I am sorry, Lord. Where I have desired the praises of people, I ask You to forgive me. Help me to have a heavenly perspective. Show me the eternal benefits of keeping my heart right before You. Purify my heart, I pray, in Jesus' name. Amen.

TODAY'S TWEET:

I live to please my heavenly Father.
#detoxforyoursoul

DAY 19

Distractions

"Keep your eyes straight ahead; ignore all sideshow distractions."
—Proverbs 4:25 (MSG)

The Bible contains an answer for every problem in life. If you are afraid, the Word points you to the One who is your Security. If you are sick, there are verses to instruct you in healing. If you are broke, the Bible will teach you how to prosper. If you are burdened, the Scriptures will show you the route to emotional and mental relief. The devil recognizes the power of God's Word to solve your problems, so he does everything imaginable to try to stop you from studying it. And one of his most trusted weapons is distraction. If a world-class tennis player competing in a match continually took his eye off the ball, he would not win the match—no matter how talented he was. Similarly, if we consistently lose our true focus, we will live a life of missed opportunities and unfulfilled dreams. We will not achieve our potential.

In an earlier message, we discussed Jesus' parable about a sower planting seed in the ground. Some seed produced a bumper crop, but other seed did not. Jesus shared this story to help us understand the devil's tactics and to ensure that our seed would be fruitful. Let's apply this parable to our relationship with God's Word. The "sower" is your pastor's sermon, or the book you are reading, or your own study of the Bible. The "seed" is the Word of God. The "soil" represents your heart. Depending on the state of your heart, the Word will either bring spiritual growth and success or be rendered powerless.

*And the ones sown among the thorns are others who hear the Word;
then the cares and anxieties of the world and* **distractions of the age,**
*and the pleasure and delight and false glamour and deceitfulness of
riches, and the* **craving and passionate desire for other things** *creep
in and choke and suffocate the Word, and it becomes fruitless.*

(Mark 4:18–19 AMP)

Why do you think Jesus compared life's distractions with thorns?
Thorns can scratch and cut. The issues of your life might steal your attention because they irritate or hurt you.

Putting Daily Demands in Perspective

When my daughter Abby was young, she contended with major medical
challenges. She was in and out of hospital and was often in pain. It is always
hard to see someone you love suffer. When it is your child, it can be particularly difficult. It was not long before the disease became a distraction to me. I
was thinking more about appointments and pain relief than I was about the
things of God. My daughter's ailments became the center of my world.

In His mercy, God showed me my error. I went to Him in prayer, repented, and rededicated my daughter into His healing hands. Of course,
I continued to care for her, but my heart was free of clutter. I continued to
deal with daily demands, yet they were not my focus. Disease is already an
enemy of ours. If Satan can use sickness to sidetrack us, too, he is doubling
the power of disease to hinder us.

Distractions can come in various forms. I know too many stories of
people who have fervently prayed for promotion in the workplace, but
when they got a new job, they didn't come to church as often as they used
to. Others have taken promotions that have forced them to work every
Sunday. They end up craving success more than they desire the fulfillment
of their God-given destiny. Work, work, work! Their priority becomes ob-
taining the next pay raise, getting that important training, or winning a
new contract. However, true fulfillment will come only from accomplishing God's purposes. To grow in God, we must study His Word, and we
need to be part of a local church family. The Lord wants you to do well,

and He longs to promote you. However, His plan is that you will prosper in natural things to the extent that you prosper in spiritual things. (See 3 John 2.) When you prioritize growing in God, He will make sure that you have the things you desire. (See Matthew 6:33.)

Mark 4:19 (AMP) says that distractions, cares, false pleasures, and the deceitfulness of riches *"creep in."* They build up gradually, catching us off guard. My son reliably informs me (who knows how he knows!) that the way to boil a frog to death without the creature noticing is to place it in a pan of cold water, put the pan on a stovetop burner, and then gradually increase the heat underneath. For the record, I have never boiled a frog—but I take my son's word for it! That is exactly how Satan works. He gradually "turns up the heat" in our lives. It is easy for us to allow daily tasks to gain greater significance than they should, so that they soon become mountains to us. Hospital visits, investing hours in a business venture, practicing for a marathon, preparing for a promotion, studying for classes—before we know it, such tasks are taking too much of our time and attention. They steal the Word from us. Eventually, they choke the life out of our relationship with God. All too often, by the time we realize it, our love for the Lord has grown cold, and we no longer have the spiritual hunger to get our life back in order. That is why we must watch over our life like a hawk.

Avoiding Entanglement

No one engaged in warfare entangles himself with the affairs of this life, that he may please him who enlisted him as a soldier. (2 Timothy 2:4)

It is when our hearts and thoughts are *entangled* in life's affairs that we become distracted. Perhaps you are preoccupied with finding a spouse or with getting your children the right education. Maybe you are engrossed in your career, or you are constantly fighting various battles in your life. Jesus lived with the pressures of life all around Him, but He "set His face like flint" toward accomplishing His purpose. (See, for example, Isaiah 50:6–7; Luke 9:51–53.) You were uniquely designed to fulfill a special mandate while you are here on earth. It is only when you are pursuing God's purpose for your life that you will know the exhilaration of true fulfillment.

Outside that, you might well end up joining a rock-and-roll band and sing-ing a not-so-happy song: "I Can't Get No Satisfaction!"

The Greek word translated as *"distractions"* in Mark 4:19 (AMP) is *merimna*, which comes from a root word that connects *merimna* with the idea of a "divided mind" or double-mindedness due to the effects of cares or anxiety. Half our thoughts are on the right things, while the other half are being led astray. When we allow the issues of our lives to clutter our thoughts, we can go off in the wrong direction.

> *Be very careful to act exactly as* GOD *commands you. Don't veer off to the right or the left.*   (Deuteronomy 5:32 MSG)

God has a tremendous plan for your life, but the only way to its ful-fillment is focus. We all have many matters that keep us busy. The key is to not allow them to become our preoccupation. When we keep our eyes on the Provider, we will not lack anything. When we worship the Healer, all will be well. When we exalt the Promoter, we will be raised up in due season. When we keep our eyes on God's Word, we will grow beyond mea-sure. Success will be inevitable.

TO DO TODAY

What is stealing your time or attention away from God and His Word? Is there one big issue that distracts you, or several smaller matters? Determine if anything is preoccupying you or diverting your focus from the Lord. Consider your involvements with your family members, your work, your ministry, your hobbies, and so forth. Write down any aspect of your life that is getting in the way of your relationship with God and bring it to Him in prayer. If you realize that you need to rearrange your time or to lay down one or two activities for the sake of your future, make the change today.

PRAYER

My loving Father,

I realize that things in my life have distracted me from You. I have become preoccupied and have lost my true focus. [*Tell the*

Lord what has sidetracked you. Explain what you have had on your mind and the matters to which you have been giving too much time.] I ask You to forgive me, Lord. I bring every issue to You. I entrust every plan and purpose in my life into Your hands once more. If there are things that I am doing that are not of You, show me, Lord, and I will do what You tell me to do. I will lay down anything You ask me to give up. I will take up anything You ask me to focus on. I will obey the leading of Your Spirit.

Now I set my heart and my mind on You and focus anew on Your priorities. Thank You that You have my best interests at heart. When I put my life in Your hands, I am in the safest place. When I leave my career in Your care, I will fulfill my potential. Keep me focused on You and Your purposes for me. In Jesus' name, amen.

TODAY'S TWEET:

My heavenly Father's priorities are my priorities.
#detoxforyoursoul

DAY 20

Striving for Success

"A man's gift makes room for him, and brings him before great men."
—Proverbs 18:16

Being married to a pastor can be a challenge. For some reason, people often define you by your husband's role. When my husband and I started out in ministry, I was often introduced to people in this way: "Meet Jo. She is a pastor's wife." I have friends who are married to doctors, lawyers, journalists, mechanics, missionaries, and so on, yet they are not labeled according to their partners' jobs. It shouldn't matter how we are described, but it used to bother me. I would try to prove that I was not *just* a wife. When we hosted guest speakers, I wanted to show them my value, so I would contribute to the conversation by telling stories that demonstrated my talents. Yet, inside, I was crying out, *I'm not a nobody. I'm somebody!* When it eventually occurred to me that farmers' wives have the same issue, I wanted to drive into the country, knock on random farmhouse doors until I found a woman who was married to a farmer, grab her, give her a big hug, and shout, "Yes, I understand you!"

No Need to Prove Ourselves to Others

The problem is, Jesus modeled a very different attitude. Paul wrote about Him,

Who, although being essentially one with God and in the form of God [possessing the fullness of the attributes which make God God], did

not think this equality with God was a thing to be eagerly grasped or retained, but stripped Himself [of all privileges and rightful dignity], so as to assume the guise of a servant (slave)....

(Philippians 2:6–7 AMP)

Jesus never clamored for position or prominence. He did not cling to His privileges or His power. He knew who He was, so He never felt the need to prove anything to anyone. And God the Father values you and me just as much as He values Jesus. We do not need to strive for equality with other people. We do not have to shout to be heard.

I had thought I had to fight my way to fulfillment, and I was constantly trying to climb higher. But the Lord started to deal with my heart, showing me that I had grappled for recognition. So, I prayed. I told God how sorry I was for trying to do things in my own strength, for trying to promote myself. I determined that I would no longer strive for success. My life was (and is) in His hands. I wanted His way or no way.

Trapped Talents

Perhaps promoting yourself is the last thing you would do, because you have given up on your God-given gifts. Maybe you are like the prophet Jonah—reluctant at every turn. You do not want to draw attention to yourself, so you hide your light. God created each of us for a unique purpose, and He has given us talents that we need to use to fulfill our destiny.

When He ascended on high, He led captivity captive, and gave gifts to men.   (Ephesians 4:8)

God wants you to use the gifts He has given you for His glory. One of the saddest things to discover is that the talents God has given to His people have not been used but have remained trapped in their hearts. Sometimes, our gifts lie dormant because we won't overcome our character flaws, such as stubbornness or jealousy. At other times, they are limited by our reluctance to come out of the shadows and be used by the Lord. The Bible says that every one of us has a role:

*The whole body, joined and knit together by what **every joint supplies**, according to the effective working by which **every part does its share**, causes growth of the body....*   (Ephesians 4:16)

Don't allow intimidation or inertia to hold you back. Every one of us has to overcome something in order to succeed. Four times, God told His new leader, Joshua, to be brave. (See Deuteronomy 31:23; Joshua 1:6, 7, 9.) In the same way, you and I need to do what it takes to make our lives count. Make a determined decision to set free God's gift in you in order to help others. Then let the Lord work in *His* way. He wants you to fulfill your destiny. If you obey His Word and keep your heart right, He will promote you at the appointed time.

For promotion cometh neither from the east, nor from the west, nor from the south. But God is the judge: he putteth down one, and setteth up another.   (Psalm 75:6–7 KJV)

An Open Door Before Us

It often drains a person to run around trying to make things happen in his or her own strength. Believe me, I know this from exhausting personal experience! You do not have to battle to be noticed—the God-given gifts in you will open doors at the right time. All the Lord seeks from you and me is humility and obedience. As today's key verse says, *"A man's gift makes room for him, and brings him before great men."*

All too often, when nothing is going our way, we try to make things happen. For example, we may push for promotion. The Bible tells us that God has set before us an *open* door. (See Revelation 3:8.) That means that we won't need to smash down *closed* doors. (In reality, these are more likely to be trap doors!) There are other times when we throw in the towel and ignore wide-open doors just because carrying on is difficult. Neither approach is the answer.

Do not be like the horse or like the mule, which have no understanding.   (Psalm 32:9)

Like a horse that is always chomping at the bit, some of us have a propensity for running ahead of God by pushing and striving. We need to recognize this trait in ourselves and learn to wait for His timing and His leading. By contrast, the mule drags its feet. It is slow and passive and seeks the path of least resistance. If you are like the mule, you will need to learn to stir yourself up and lay hold of God's promises. Eradicate procrastination from your life by making a decision to do now—not later—what needs to be done.

Whichever animal's behavior you emulate, you will need to be watchful in both directions. Although I am more of a "horse" than a "mule," there are times when I have felt like giving up. One year, I took my laptop on holiday with me, and I found myself writing during every free moment. Two days before we returned, my husband shared his disappointment that I had spent more time with my computer than with him. I felt terrible. I said I was sorry and put my work away. When we got home, I was reluctant to write. I had messed up, so I did not want to pick up my book again. I was behaving like a mule.

Do not neglect the gift [of God] *that is in you.*   (1 Timothy 4:14)

Perhaps, as I did, you have tried to promote your own gifts. Or maybe you have given up on your gifts. God asks one thing of us: to follow His leading. For some people, it is time to stop striving for success. For others, it is time to pick up God's plans once again and to *"stir up the gift"* (2 Timothy 1:6) within them.

TO DO TODAY

Are you a "horse" or a "mule"? Do you try to "break down doors," or do you hold back? If you know you have a propensity for running ahead of God, acknowledge that inclination before the Lord today. Review each area of your life, including your work and/or your ministry. Are you striving in any of these areas? Lay down any man-made plans and instead listen for God's leading. Don't force doors—wait for them to be opened.

If you know you drag your feet, think about the various areas of your life, including your work and/or your ministry. Is there anything you should be doing that you have laid aside, neglected, or ignored? Do you keep putting off until tomorrow what you know you should do today? Ask the Holy Spirit to show you the one or two tasks that He is asking you to pick up again now. Do one thing today toward their fulfillment and make time in your schedule to ensure their completion.

PRAYER

My loving Father,

I realize there are times when I have promoted myself. I have sought success and have tried to force doors to open. I have been desperate for recognition and have attempted to advertise my gifts. I am sorry, and I ask You to forgive me. I lay down my life before You again. I am in Your hands. I submit to Your timing and Your ways.

Where I have given up on the dreams You have given me, or where I have been slow to obey, I apologize. Where I have become discouraged, I ask You to heal my heart and to restore my vision. I stir up the gifts You have given to me. I put my hands back on the plow and begin again. Your Word says that the sons (and daughters) of God are led by the Spirit of God, so I ask You to lead me. In Jesus' name, amen.

TODAY'S TWEET:

I want God's way or no way. #detoxforyoursoul

Step 3

BUILD UP

DAY 21

Frame Your Future

"Those who control their tongue will have a long life; opening your mouth can ruin everything."
—Proverbs 13:3 (NLT)

At the beginning of time, God showed us the purpose of speech. In the midst of darkness and chaos, the Lord spoke light and life. He created a magnificent world by the power of His words. And, when He designed you and me, He made us in His image.

Then God said, "Let Us make man in Our image, according to Our likeness." (Genesis 1:26)

Just as God's speech has great authority, so our words have real power. The Lord's plan is that our conversation would bring about salvation, healing, and hope. He wants us to use our words in the way He uses His—to create life and to sustain it. Our tongues affect our lives—for good, if our speech is full of faith and love; or for bad, if we talk negatively. Our mouths are so powerful that the enemy works overtime to try to fill them with words of doubt and criticism.

Death and life are in the power of the tongue. (Proverbs 18:21)

Our Tongues Have an Important Job

The Hebrew word for *"power"* in the above verse literally means "hand." If I leave a project in your hands, I am delegating the responsibility for it to you. Similarly, our tongues have been given an important job to carry out. They are responsible, to a large extent, for how things in our lives turn out. My words can bring joy, peace, healing, and love into my life. Alternatively, my words can lead to death and everything linked to it: sin, sickness, hate, and fear.

When I was a child, if someone cursed, that person was told to clean out his or her mouth with soap! I believe we should cleanse our conversation so that we have the best chance of a great life. You might not use crude words. However, you might be using another sort of "bad language." When we are spiritually dry or discouraged, we can all too easily develop negative patterns of speech. Matthew 12:34 says that *out of the abundance of the heart the mouth speaks.* So, when we are feeling down, we often end up "talking down." Unfortunately, that normally makes things even worse for us.

> *You are snared by the words of your mouth; you are taken by the words of your mouth.* (Proverbs 6:2)

"Snared" means trapped. If I do not watch what I say, my words can lead me into the devil's trap. If I am already in a difficult place, careless comments can tighten Satan's grip. It can be tempting to say the wrong stuff.

Imagine that you have been praying for a breakthrough. However, things just seem to get worse, and you want to let your frustration out, saying things such as "It's never going to happen"; "Everyone else is getting their breakthrough, but I am stuck in a rut"; "My husband is a monster, my kids are driving me mad, and I cannot stand this stupid job!"

The Bible teaches us that we get what we say:

> *Whoever **says** to this mountain, "Be removed and be cast into the sea," and does not doubt in his heart, but believes that those things he **says** will be done, **he will have whatever he says**.* (Mark 11:23)

If I *say* that I will never get my breakthrough, there is a chance that I will receive what I have confessed. If I *say* that my prayers never get answered, then the devil has every excuse to block the fulfillment of God's promises in my life. You and I need to make sure that what we say *after* we have prayed lines up with what we said *while* we were praying. If I thanked God in prayer that He would meet my needs according to His riches in glory, then, when I am chatting with a friend later that day, I need to agree with my faith-filled prayers! Why? Because the Bible says that we have what we *say*, not just what we *pray*.

Keep Trusting!

The Bible rarely puts a delivery date on its promises. God told seventy-five-year-old Abraham that he would have a son. Nevertheless, the father of faith had to wait twenty-five years for the birth of Isaac. Abraham believed God in spite of the delay. In the same way, our job is to keep trusting, no matter how long it takes. Hebrews 6:12 says that by faith *and* patience, we inherit our promises. What we say is the greatest evidence of what we believe. At the same time, what we say shapes *what* we believe. So, by choosing to declare, "It might be hard right now, but I know that God is at work and that His promises will be fulfilled in my life," you will be strengthening your faith with your words—instead of tearing it down. Even if you need to put your hand over your mouth, do not let words of doubt come out!

> *Whoever guards his mouth and tongue keeps his soul from troubles.*
> (Proverbs 21:23)

By dropping negative thoughts into your mind, Satan tries to get you to say the wrong things. You need to conquer those harmful thoughts with positive words. If you are thinking, *I cannot stand this anymore*, fight back by declaring, *"I can do all things through Christ who strengthens me"* (Philippians 4:13). Just as you would use your steering wheel to maneuver your car out of danger, use your words to propel yourself out of difficulty. As our key Scripture for today says,

> *Those who control their tongue will have a long life; opening your mouth can ruin everything.*

Your Tongue Determines Your Course

The third chapter of James teaches us that the tongue is like the rudder of a ship or the bit in a horse's mouth. Both devices control direction. What we say will determine our course. If you are constantly saying that you are "sick of this" or "sick of that," please don't be too surprised if you frequently become ill! When people ask you how you are, use it as an opportunity to declare God's goodness. Saying "I'm doing great" will help you far more than saying "Not too bad." Make a decision that you will tame your tongue with the Holy Spirit's help.

The heart of the wise teaches his mouth….   (Proverbs 16:23)

Just as with training an animal, training the tongue does not happen overnight. However, if you work at it, you will become a little more disciplined each day. Several years ago, I felt constantly tired and overwhelmed. I was a wife, a mum, a minister, and a vice president at a leading PR firm, so I had a lot going on. I knew I was in the will of God and that I should not be feeling so weary. I understood the power of words, so I decided that I would not allow "busy" or "tired" to come out of my mouth. I no longer confessed exhaustion but instead said that I was getting stronger all the time. I stopped saying I had too much going on and instead said that life was full but enjoyable. The transformation was almost immediate. Stress dropped from my shoulders, and vitality returned. I was more than capable. I just needed my mouth to line up with God's purposes.

"To bless" means to confer benefits, and "to curse" means to pronounce harm. We bless when we speak positively about ourselves (or someone else). We inadvertently curse when we speak negatively. Let us use our words to build our future, not to tear it down.

I have set before you life and death, blessing and cursing; therefore choose life, that both you and your descendants may live.
(Deuteronomy 30:19)

Choose to breathe life into your dryness. Make a decision to speak love into your marriage. Agree with God's Word that He is mending your broken heart or healing your body. Pronounce that God's power is bringing restoration to your family, your ministry, your business, or your work. Let us break out of negativity and use our mouths for good.

TO DO TODAY

Choose one area of your life in which you are believing God for a breakthrough. Search God's Word for a promise about your situation. Write out your verse and start confessing it daily. In addition, decide to speak *only* in faith concerning this matter. Hold your tongue any time you want to complain or doubt. See what God will do.

PRAYER

My loving Father,

I am sorry for the wrong things that I have said about my life and about my future. [*If there are specific negative things that you have often said, tell the Lord.*] I ask You to forgive me for every idle, doubting, or negative word that I have spoken. Cleanse my heart and purify my mouth, I pray. From today forward, I will use my tongue to breathe life into situations. I will declare words of light when I feel the darkness closing in. I will speak hope when Satan tries to make me despair. I will encourage myself when I feel down. I will remind myself of God's promises when doubt lurks. I choose life, and I choose to bless! In Jesus' mighty name, amen.

TODAY'S TWEET:

I will use my tongue to steer myself out of difficulty & into God's purposes. #detoxforyoursoul

DAY 22

Love Is the Way

"Love covers all sins."
—Proverbs 10:12

Many years ago, I went on a ministry trip to Scotland. Our hosts inspired me: After twenty-four years of marriage, four children, and several grandchildren, they still acted like newlyweds. The pastor pinched his wife's bottom when he thought no one was looking. They giggled and often held hands. I asked what their secret was, and I have never forgotten their words: "Love is not about give-and-take. Love is about 'give-and-give.'"

In our society, it's easy to think that love is merely a warm feeling that makes us glow, or something like empathy that others should express to us when we are in need. However, because God loved, He *gave*. Love is something we do. It is how we treat people. It is a way of life.

Love is patient and kind. Love is not jealous or boastful or proud or rude. It does not demand its own way. It is not irritable, and it keeps no record of being wronged. (1 Corinthians 13:4–5 NLT)

Love bears up under anything and everything that comes, is ever ready to believe the best of every person.... (1 Corinthians 13:7 AMP)

These verses define love. As you read the "love checklist" below, think about how you treat the people around you—your family members, your friends, your colleagues, church folk, shopkeepers, cab drivers, and so on. Where do you meet the mark, and where do you need to grow in love?

Ten Traits of Love

1. *Patient:* Bearing with people when they are annoying. Not pushing ahead of others. Not being irritable or snappish. Allowing folk the time they need to do things.

2. *Kind:* Being gracious and thoughtful. Doing good to people who aren't good to you—people who do not deserve it.

3. *Positive:* Believing the best about friends and family members, and seeing the good in others when it is hard to find.

4. *Not jealous:* Feeling genuinely happy when other people excel and when opponents succeed.

5. *Not boastful:* Never blowing your own trumpet or drawing attention to yourself but celebrating others, instead.

6. *Not proud:* Happily serving people who seem less important than you are. Having a teachable attitude and a tender heart.

7. *Not rude:* Demonstrating graciousness when, for example, waiters mess up or salespeople make mistakes. Showing courtesy to other drivers, irrespective of their apparent incompetence!

8. *Not demanding:* Readily and regularly letting others have their way, for love's sake.

9. *Not irritable:* Not easily provoked by friends or family members (or even gruff parking attendants!).

10. *Not a point-scorer:* Forgetting the wrongs that others have committed and giving people the benefit of the doubt.

Gold that is genuine is identified by a hallmark. Similarly, love demonstrates the genuineness of our faith. Jesus said, "If you love one another, everyone will know that you are My disciples." (See John 13:35.)

Recently, I made a light, throwaway comment to a friend in my neighborhood, and she shouted at me and then stormed off. I ran after her to apologize and followed that up with a telephone call to check to see if she was OK. She barked at me again, telling me that I was rude. I was shocked and hurt by the disproportionate onslaught. Although it was hard to do so,

I held my peace for love's sake. I did not defend myself or question her reaction. I simply told her that I was very sorry and greeted her with a smile the next time I saw her.

He who covers a transgression seeks love. (Proverbs 17:9)

When we love, we cover up the wrongs of others with our kindness. We overlook their mistakes and treat them with warmth. We are gracious and patient. There is no strife in love, so it feels good to live in a loving way. It not only demonstrates goodness to others, but it also helps us to maintain peace within ourselves.

Therefore be imitators of God as dear children. And walk in love, as Christ also has loved us and given Himself for us, an offering and a sacrifice to God for a sweet-smelling aroma. (Ephesians 5:1–2)

A Way of Life

Again, love is something we *do*, not something we *feel*. It is a choice, not a reaction. As I wrote earlier, it is a way of life. It is also often a sacrifice. The carnal nature *reacts* to the issues of others, whereas our renewed nature *responds* to them. The flesh wants to lash out, but love restrains us so that we can be gracious and kind.

Christ's love controls us. (2 Corinthians 5:14 NLT)

As with any skill that we want to perfect, we need to practice love. We can work at improving the way we treat others, such as shopkeepers, waiters, and stewards. The more kindness and patience we sow into other people's lives, the more kindness and patience we will reap. Getting used to being generous toward strangers will make it easier for us to walk in love at home.

The love of God has been poured out in our hearts. (Romans 5:5)

The Lord has already deposited His love in the bank of our hearts. We just need to withdraw it and then share it. God is love, so the more we give love, the more we resemble Him.

Henry and Paul were friends. One afternoon, when a sizeable group of young men and women were gathered together, Henry started to "prophesy" over Paul. I have put that word in quotation marks because what he did was not what the Bible means by prophesy—which is to edify, encourage, and exhort. Henry spoke as though his words came directly from God and said that Paul was full of arrogance and pride, that his motives were warped, and that if he did not repent, God would judge him. Paul felt humiliated and hurt by the harshness of Henry's words. He left the meeting embarrassed and alone.

Despite his pain, Paul decided to walk in love. Aware that Henry was in financial difficulty, Paul visited the local supermarket, bought him three bags of groceries, and dropped them off at his apartment. He then went on his way. He did not think much more about the matter. The next time Paul saw Henry was at a dinner party a few months later. Halfway through the meal, Henry stood to his feet and shared, "I just want to thank Paul. Everything I have learned about love, I have learned from this man." Then he sat down.

The room was quiet. A young woman looked on amazed and was deeply touched by Henry's words. So, when Paul asked her on a date, she felt certain that he must be a very honorable person, and she agreed. I was that young woman. That evening was the first time I met my husband. The rest, as they say, is history! Of course, walking in love does not always lead you to the man or woman of your dreams, but it will always lead you to victory.

But above all these things put on love, which is the bond of perfection.
(Colossians 3:14)

Maturity isn't how much we know; it is how much love we show. According to 1 Corinthians 13, it is the ultimate sign of Christian growth. Our maturity is demonstrated by how patient, kind, and affirming we are to the people around us. A friend once told me that she faked love until she felt it! I suggest you do the same. Demonstrate love, and eventually your feelings will catch up with it.

To be "baptized" means to be submerged or soaked. I believe that we need to be baptized in God's love. He wants to wash away all our impatience, irritability, and self-centeredness so that we can share His wonderful nature with others.

TO DO TODAY

Evaluate yourself using the 1 Corinthians 13 checklist. On a scale from 1 to 10 (10 being highest), how much do you demonstrate each of the attributes of love when you are around difficult people? Which particular trait do you need to develop the most? Start practicing it deliberately. Tell a friend what you are doing and ask him or her to help you keep on the right track.

PRAYER

My loving Father,

You love me unconditionally, and I want to do for others what You do for me. I am sorry for the times when I have been impatient or unkind. I apologize for those instances when I have been rude or judgmental. [*If the Lord has convicted you of any specific shortcomings, confess them.*]

Your Word says that just as Christ laid down His life for us, so we should lay down our lives for our brothers and sisters. I should be living to love, not living to be loved. I ask You to fill me afresh with Your Spirit. Baptize me in Your wonderful love. I put on love, and I ask for Your help as I practice loving others. In Jesus' name, amen.

TODAY'S TWEET:

Maturity isn't how much I know; it's how much love I show. #detoxforyoursoul

DAY 23

Yes, Sir!

"The wise in heart will accept and obey commandments."
—Proverbs 10:8 (AMP)

If you were raised in a democratic society, you will be accustomed to having your say, or speaking your mind. Under many democracies, students and parents have the ability to challenge teachers. Unions are allowed to form in places of business in order to speak and act on behalf of the employees and to secure their rights. Politicians are held accountable to the people who voted to put them in office. Recently, while attending a wedding in the nation of Denmark, I witnessed a shining example of democracy. The wedding was so democratic that everyone wanted to make a speech. Five-and-a-half hours later, nearly every guest had had his or her say, and the rest of us were frazzled!

After living in a democratic, independent environment, some people feel they should "have their say" all the time! Thanks to the sacrifice of Jesus, we have access to the Father of all creation. We can boldly approach the throne of almighty God to worship Him and to ask for His help in time of need. (See Hebrews 4:16.) The Bible says His sheep (that's us) know His voice and are led by His Spirit. (See John 10:27.) So, if we have access to the King of all creation, and we can hear God for ourselves, why should we submit to people here on earth? To answer this question, let's look at two examples from the Word.

Greatness Comes from Living Under Authority

First, in the New Testament, Jesus was very impressed by a Roman centurion who understood the concept of authority. The centurion said to Him,

For I also am a man [daily] subject to authority, with soldiers under me. And I say to one, Go, and he goes; and to another, Come, and he comes; and to my bond servant, Do this, and he does it.

(Luke 7:8 AMP)

This high-ranking military officer subjected himself to authority on a daily basis. He readily received, accepted, and obeyed commands. He did not pause for thought to see if he first agreed with an order. He did what he was told. Because of his submission, he was given great authority over others.

In the Old Testament, Elisha was destined for greatness. He probably knew from his youth that the hand of God was upon him. Just as David learned to know God while mastering his skills as a shepherd, so Elisha learned to hear God's voice while training to be a farmer. When he grew older, Elisha's leadership skills were demonstrated as he developed a successful agricultural business. Mighty ministries are not made overnight. They are developed over decades. By the time Elisha met the prophet Elijah, he was competent and mature. Yet he willingly gave up being his own boss in order to serve the prophet:

Then he arose and followed Elijah, and became his servant.

(1 Kings 19:21)

Elisha did not become Elijah's deputy or executive assistant. He became his servant. He followed instructions. I am sure there were times when Elisha had a better idea than what he was told to do. Nevertheless, he understood authority, and he did what Elijah said.

I believe that one of the tests we have to pass in order to be promoted by God to the level of our true potential is the obedience test. I am not talking about our need to submit to Scripture or to follow the leading of God's voice (although both are vital). I am referring to the ability to do what another human being who is in authority over us tells us to do.

*The wise in heart will **receive** commands.* (Proverbs 10:8)

This verse is striking. Surely, the wise would be the most qualified to question commands, wouldn't they? After all, they know more than most. You may think, *I can hear from God myself. I can make my own decisions.* Yes, I am sure you can. Yet Scripture says that the wise will accept and readily receive orders. You see, willingness is a measure of our humility—not of our spiritual ability. And it gauges our readiness for greatness. When I huff and puff or flatly refuse to listen to those in authority, it shows the condition of my heart. It reveals that I am probably not ready for prominence. Yet, when I am quick to listen and to obey, then I am well on the way.

Submission Releases God's Authority

When my boss (who also happens to be my husband) asks me to lay down my carefully crafted and prayed-over plans, it measures the extent of my surrender. When he asks me to do something I don't want to do, it tests my humility. Our church auditorium has a range of TV lights. I am not a technician, so I never really took the time to learn how to operate them. One Sunday, before I was due to preach, my husband asked me to switch on some additional lamps. I was only about two feet closer to the system than he was, so I thought to myself, *Why on earth can't you do it yourself? I am about to preach!*

However, aware that attitude is everything, I bit my lip, walked over to the system, and worked it out. Then I returned to my seat. "It's pointing in the wrong direction," my husband promptly informed me. So, looking back at him, this time with raised eyebrows, I returned to adjust the direction. I found my seat again and shut my eyes. I was getting back into God's presence when he interrupted me another time. "It's flickering!" I felt like strangling him with my bare hands! After all, I was the important one that day because I was preaching—not he! Thankfully, by this time, I realized this whole thing was a test. So, I smiled oh so sweetly (through gritted teeth, if the truth be known) and adjusted the lights until they were perfect. I reminded myself that he was my boss, as well as my husband, and then thanked him (with a slightly wry smile on my face) for the timely training!

Since then, I have worked hard to do what I'm told with an attitude of humility. God has put two or three leaders in my life. Even though I am a pastor and a preacher, I have learned to be quick to consent if these leaders ask me to do something. Submitting to others releases God's authority in my life.

> *He who is greatest among you shall be your servant. Whoever exalts himself [with haughtiness and empty pride] shall be humbled (brought low), and whoever humbles himself [whoever has a modest opinion of himself and behaves accordingly] shall be raised to honor.*
> (Matthew 23:11–12 AMP)

This verse does not say, "He who is greatest among you shall be *My* servant." It says, "*He who is greatest among you shall be* **your** *servant.*" It is one thing to do what God says. It is something else to do what a brother or sister whom God has appointed over you says. That takes humility—and it is a key to promotion. Jesus is Lord of all, yet He came to earth as a Servant and did what He was told to do by His Father. He did not say what He chose to say; He spoke only what He heard from His Father. His will was subject to God the Father's will at all times. He did not seek to please Himself. He sought to please only the Father.

> [Jesus] *humbled Himself and became obedient....* (Philippians 2:8)

The Son of God demonstrated His humility through His obedience. He always listened to His Father and always did what the Father said. And, when Jesus was training His followers for leadership, He taught them to submit to one another.

The ability to take orders is a quality demonstrated by many Bible heroes. Moses heeded the advice of his father-in-law, even though he himself was the "man of God." (See Exodus 18:13–26.) King David, Israel's greatest leader, heeded a rebuke from Nathan the prophet when he could have had him killed, instead. (See 2 Samuel 12:1–15.) Ruth did what Naomi instructed her, even though it required great boldness. (See Ruth 3.) Esther followed her uncle's instructions, even though she was the queen. (See Esther 4.) The apostles learned from each other as the early church grew. (See, for example, Acts 11:1–18.) The way up really is the way down.

TO DO TODAY

Who is your "Elijah"? Has God put a leader, a mentor, or a pastor in your life? If you do not know whom to serve, then ask God to show you. We are all called to submit ourselves to someone else. That is one of the greatest ways for God to work on our character. If you already know whom God wants you to support, then make a decision today to help that person in his or her endeavors. Offer your assistance wherever it is needed—even if the job is not glamorous and will not be accompanied by any recognition. God will surely raise you up.

PRAYER

My loving Father,

Thank You that You have called me to make a difference in this life and that You are teaching me to yield to You and to other people. Where I have found it difficult to obey, I humble myself. Where I have struggled to submit, I choose to surrender. I make a decision to listen to the leaders You have placed in my life. You are testing my heart—not how "spiritual" I am. You want to promote me, but the way up is down. Your Word says that Jesus took on the form of a bondservant—a slave. I want to serve just as He served—with love. In Jesus' name, I pray. Amen.

TODAY'S TWEET:

The way up is the way down. #detoxforyoursoul

DAY 24

The Test of Time

"Truthful words stand the test of time."
—Proverbs 12:19 (NLT)

God invented time. He stepped out of eternity and created hours, days, weeks, months, and years; He designed ages and seasons—all for a purpose. These measurements and environments are part of His plan for perfecting you and me.

> *Then God said, "Let there be lights in the firmament of the heavens to divide the day from the night; and let them be for signs and seasons, and for days and years."* (Genesis 1:14)

My daughter Abby battled with health problems for the first decade of her life. One day, when she was nine years old and in the middle of an uncomfortable medical procedure, she asked me, "Mummy, why hasn't God healed me yet?" She was fed up with pain and weary of waiting. She wanted everything with her to be normal, and she did not want to suffer any additional symptoms. She felt forgotten. We talked together and then hugged. She cried, and I reminded her of every miracle that God had already done to bring her to that place safe and well. We went back to God's promises in Scripture. She was ready to fight again.

Waiting and Preparing

One of the reasons we often have to wait is that God wants to give us our breakthrough when we are fully ready to walk in His promises. There is a remarkable little boy in our church named Michael. When he was just two, his parents went to a local supermarket. His dad ran inside to buy some groceries while Emma, his mum, waited in the car. She saw an old friend, so she jumped out of the vehicle to say hello. Michael was still sitting in the backseat. A few moments later, Emma nearly jumped out of her skin when the car, which she had been leaning on, suddenly sprang to life, with the engine revving like it was about to take off! Little Michael had unfastened his seat belt, climbed into the front seat, leaned forward, and turned the key in the ignition. Fortunately, that's as far as it went. Michael had a phenomenal flair for driving but was certainly not ready for the roads! He needed much more growth, preparation, and skill.

At the age of twelve, Jesus proved Himself in ministry when He sat and spoke with the teachers of the law in the temple. (See Luke 2:41–49.) Nonetheless, He did not begin His ministry until He was thirty. (See Luke 3:23.) For eighteen years, Jesus waited and prepared. Then He spent three years training His team of twelve disciples. He worked on their character and built their faith. He taught them to preach and trained them to minister. He was raising up future leaders. Then, before He ascended to heaven, He revealed to them that the biggest revival in history was about to break out.

> [Jesus] *commanded them not to depart from Jerusalem, but to wait for the Promise of the Father, "which," He said, "you have heard from Me; for John truly baptized with water, but you shall be baptized with the Holy Spirit not many days from now."* (Acts 1:4–5)

Jesus was telling His disciples that their breakthrough was imminent. I am sure that their excitement was building and their expectations were high. Joel's prophecy was about to be fulfilled, and they would be witnesses of Jesus. (See Acts 1:8.) In both the *New Living Translation* and the *New International Version*, Acts 1:5 says that the disciples would be baptized with the Holy Spirit in *"a few days."* To most of us, "a few days" means two or three days—at the most, four or five.

Yet, the first week came and went, and nothing happened. The disciples stayed in the upper room, wondering and waiting. (See Acts 1:12–14.)

Week two passed. People were probably starting to doubt, saying, "What if Jesus didn't mean what He said? Maybe we didn't hear Him right. Or perhaps we have done something wrong." They may well have started to blame each other. "Peter, it's your fault. You denied Jesus. You've blown it for all of us."

Week three. Some followers may have given up and gone back home. But those who remained must have pulled together, affirming, "Jesus said it, so Jesus will do it. We just need to stay, pray, and believe."

Week four. Perhaps this is when Peter had a flash of inspiration. "I know why the Holy Spirit has not yet fallen. We are missing a man! We need to select an apostle to replace Judas. Until we do, nothing else will happen." So, the disciples cast lots, and Matthias was chosen. "Now we're ready." (See Acts 1:15–26.) Nevertheless, the wait continued. Have you ever been sure that you had identified the reason for the delay of something you were expecting? As a result, you got your heart right and set your house in order. Yet the wait continued. That does not mean you were wrong. You were probably closer than ever to your breakthrough.

Week five. The group was smaller, but those who remained stayed strong. They shared testimonies and prayed in faith and unity.

Week six. They continued to wait. And then, after forty days—not two days, three days, or ten days, but forty—it happened!

> *When the Day of Pentecost had fully come, they were all with one accord in one place.* (Acts 2:1)

"*Fully come*" means "filled full" or "entirely completed." Everything was in place, and everyone was ready. The disciples were together with one accord. Love was reigning, and faith was strong. They were finally prepared for history's first-ever outpouring of God's Spirit.

> *And suddenly there came a sound from heaven, as of a rushing mighty wind, and it filled the whole house where they were sitting.* (Acts 2:2)

Worth the Wait

I do not know what you have been waiting for or how long you have waited. I do know that God's plan is perfect. If you are sure that what you are believing for *is* from God, it is worth the wait. Patience involves having faith in God's timing. Our patience is demonstrated when we endure delay without getting unduly disheartened. All too often, we think we are waiting for God, but, in truth, He is probably waiting for us. He is watching while we deal with our stubbornness, pride, jealousy, or insecurity. He is eagerly anticipating the time when our character is ready for our destiny. Out of His great love, He will not fulfill every promise until we are ready.

Abraham waited a quarter of a century for his promised son. Isaac prayed for two decades before his wife conceived twins. Jacob worked fourteen years for the woman he loved. Joseph withstood thirteen years of slavery and imprisonment before his dream was fulfilled. Yet, in the midst of the trials and testing, God was working His purposes *in* them so that they would be ready for Him to work His purposes *through* them. Right from the start, God was teaching His people patience.

> *Let us not grow weary while doing good, for in due season we shall reap* *if we do not lose heart.*   (Galatians 6:9)

Harvest is the season when crops are ripe. It is determined by the readiness of the plants, not by the weather. One variety of apple tree takes ten years to produce its first fruit, while other varieties bear fruit much more quickly. *"Due season"* refers to your time. It is when you are ready to receive God's promise. I believe it took thirteen years to make Joseph into a man who could lead a nation. God is never in a rush. He would rather keep a job vacant than give it to someone before he or she is ready. The key is to make sure that you do not lose heart while you are waiting. In due season, when we are fully prepared, His purposes will come to pass. By the time they do, the chances are that we will not be overwrought with impatience. We will be at peace and will not be concerned with hurrying God.

I used to be desperate for God's promises to me of a great ministry to come to pass. I would cry out to the Lord again and again, begging Him to open doors. I must have sounded like a broken record in His ears! Then I started to understand the work God still had to do in me to get me ready for my destiny. My prayers changed. "Do everything You need to do in me to ensure I am prepared for your purposes," I told Him. I became content that when my heart was ready—and not before—the right doors would swing open. I have not looked back since.

Jesus said, *"Come to me, all of you who are weary and carry heavy burdens, and I will give you rest"* (Matthew 11:28 NLT). If you are worn out, you need to go to Jesus. Tell Him you are tired and give Him your troubles. As you wait in His presence, He *will* give you rest. Then you can rebuild your faith and replenish your trust in God. Acknowledge that your life is in His hands and that you know He is dependable—and always will be. To receive our promise, we need to encourage ourselves. We need to stay strong. We need to remember and rehearse what God's Word says. *"He who promised **is** faithful"* (Hebrews 10:23), and He will do what He has said He will do. Let us trust God with *when* as well as with *what*. His time is the right time.

TO DO TODAY

What have you been waiting for? Have you become discouraged or depressed during the process? Write down the promises from God that you have been awaiting. If you are disheartened about their seeming delay, express to the Lord how you feel, then make a decision to change your mind-set. If a promise is good, it is worth waiting for! Tell the Lord that you are willing to be patient for as long as it takes as you continue to develop godly character.

PRAYER

My loving Father,

I am waiting for Your promises to come to pass. I lay down my plans and ask for Your purposes to be fulfilled. [*If you are weary, tell the Lord now. Tell Him what you have been waiting for, and for how long. Lay down the burden and receive His rest.*] I trust Your timing. I do not want to be like a horse that runs ahead of its owner or a mule that drags its feet. Prepare me for my appointed time, I pray. I am willing to wait for my due season because I trust You. I give You all the praise. In Jesus' name, amen.

TODAY'S TWEET:

God's time is the right time & the only time for me. #detoxforyoursoul

DAY 25

Dreams

"A dream fulfilled is a tree of life."
—Proverbs 13:12 (NLT)

When we have a picture in our mind of a promising future, it motivates us to achieve greater things. The word *"dream"* in today's key verse refers to the longing of the heart and to a desire that inspires. It is a God-given glimpse of tomorrow. The Lord loves to stir us with a vision. He showed childless Abraham that he would become the father of multitudes of people who would be as numerous as the stars. He promised Jacob that his descendants would own the land where he lived. He gave Joseph a snapshot of future greatness. God also sent prophets to tell kings that they were destined for prominence. Why? It was because hope inspires. A dream breathes life into a person.

Several years ago, I started to move in a fresh anointing. As I ministered in meetings, God came in His glory. People were having life-changing encounters in the presence of the Lord. It was remarkable. A few weeks into this move of the Spirit, my daughter Abby contracted a serious infection. For a couple of days, my husband and I watched her closely. Then I took her to the doctor's office, but they said it was nothing, and we were sent home. The next day, I texted my husband from work to ask how she was doing. His reply was succinct: "She has not eaten. She has not had a drink. She is not saying anything." Fear entered my heart. I rushed home from work to find her lying motionless on the sofa. I scooped her into my arms, and, when I looked into her eyes, I felt like I was staring death in the face. It had been six years since the sister she had never known had died, and I could not countenance losing another child.

We were met at the hospital by a team of doctors who were ready to treat her. Thankfully, we took our little girl home, fit as a fiddle, in a matter of days. Abby was well; my baby had lived. However, the ordeal had battered me. Something inside me had died. When I returned to ministry, the new anointing was gone.

Where there is no prophetic vision the people cast off restraint.

(Proverbs 29:18 ESV)

It is not just that hope inspires us. Without it, we become disheartened. We lack motivation and discipline. Without a vision, we trudge aimlessly through life. You and I actually need a dream in order to become our best. Unfortunately, the ups and downs of life can dampen our desire. For me, it was the trauma of Abby's illness, which almost literally took the life out of me. For you, it might be a disappointment or a delay. Perhaps you had set your heart on something, but it did not turn out the way you had wanted it to. You had hoped with all your heart, and then it had all crashed around you. It must have been hard for Abraham to continue to believe for a promised son for a quarter of a century while Sarah grew steadily older before his eyes.

After my daughter's ordeal, I went to the Lord in prayer. I fell on my face in His presence and poured out my heart like water before Him. I realized that although I had been healed of the loss of my firstborn, the fear of death had tried to take hold of me. I repented for not trusting the Lord, and I told Him I was sorry for doubting His faithfulness. Then I asked the Spirit of God to breathe new life into my soul. I felt revived and renewed. Then, after worshipping my wonderful Savior, I asked Him to restore my hopes and dreams. Passion to fulfill His purposes filled my heart again.

"Hope Against Hope"

The Bible says that after Abraham had been waiting for a very long time, he "hoped against hope." (See Romans 4:18 NASB.) Despite the human impossibility of his situation, he knew he served a God who could work wonders. He looked beyond the pain of Sarah's empty womb to the picture God had painted in his heart of a multitude of descendants. He kept faith alive within him.

> Looking unto Jesus, the author and finisher of our faith, who for the joy that was set before Him endured the cross. (Hebrews 12:2)

The promise of a better future enables us to endure pressure and delay. Jesus endured the cross "*for the joy that was set before Him.*" Joseph's dreams helped him to brave years of hardship. A vision propels us. It keeps us on track, even during times of testing.

> [The Lord said,] Write the vision and make it plain on tablets, that he may run who reads it. (Habakkuk 2:2)

A vision stirs excitement and produces energy so that we can run without growing weary. It focuses our lives and gives us the discipline to do what is required. A vision awakens desire, which is a powerful force:

> When desire has conceived, it gives birth.... (James 1:15)

Desire always seeks fulfillment. Whether for good or for evil, it propels us to break through barriers. If we feed a godly desire, it will grow and eventually give birth to something good. How do we feed it? By dreaming of what God can do in us and through us. We choose to believe that our aspirations will actually come to pass. Fuel your desire for a brighter, better future. It will motivate you when you need it most.

Dreams are the language of hope and, perhaps more important, they actually create hope. They paint a vivid picture in our heart of what life will look like once the promise is fulfilled. Hope is a confident expectation of what the Bible promises. So, the more we dream, the greater our hope. And hope is the forerunner of faith. Where there is no hope, there can be no faith. Where there is hope, faith comes alive.

> Faith is the substance of things hoped for. (Hebrews 11:1)

Faith is the currency of heaven and the main means by which we lay hold of God's promises. We need dreams to motivate ourselves and to prepare the ground for faith to achieve our God-given destiny.

May He grant you according to your heart's desire, and fulfill all your purpose. (Psalm 20:4)

God Plants His Desires in Us

The Bible says that when we delight ourselves in the Lord, He will give us the desires of our heart. (See Psalm 37:4.) I believe this means that when we draw close to God in love, He will plant the right desires inside us—those impulses that spur us on to fulfill our purpose. Perhaps your dream has faded or died. If you know it was from God, ask Him to reignite the fire in your soul. If you are not sure whether it was you or the Lord, pray for His will to be done in your life. As you pray that way, the desires that are from God will come alive.

Maybe you have never had much of a vision. Go before the Lord and ask Him to paint a picture of His purposes in your heart. Linger in His presence in worship and allow the Lord time to reveal your dream. I tell people to ask themselves one question while they are trying to understand their calling: "What moves me most?" People who are called to heal the sick are normally incensed by sickness. Those who are set aside to bring change in society are outraged by injustice. Those who are chosen to minister to the brokenhearted are filled with compassion when people are hurting. When you receive God's dreams for your life and pursue them wholeheartedly, you will find their fulfillment delightful.

A desire accomplished is sweet to the soul. (Proverbs 13:19)

TO DO TODAY

The Bible teaches us to write down our visions and to keep our dreams before our eyes. It is therefore time to put pen to paper—or fingers to keyboard. Express four or five of your greatest hopes in words and pictures, and then start to pray for them to be accomplished. Have your dreams at your fingertips and review them regularly. Keep going back to add new desires. See what God will do. The expectation of the righteous will not be cut off!

PRAYER

My loving Father,

I thank You that You have a wonderful plan for my life. You have a clear vision of my future. You want me to pursue Your dreams for me. [*If your desire has dwindled, tell the Lord. Explain why it has diminished, pouring out your heart before Him. Ask Him to heal your heart.*] I ask You to fill me afresh with heaven-sent hope. Where I have doubted, I am sorry. Where I have drifted from Your purposes, I repent. Where I have lost focus, help me, I pray. As I delight myself in You, plant Your desires in my heart. As You give me a vision for my life, show me how to prepare myself. Have Your way, I pray. In Jesus' name, amen.

TODAY'S TWEET:

I hope in God, so I will not be disappointed. #detoxforyoursoul

DAY 26

Strength

"She girds herself with strength…."
—Proverbs 31:17

The hardest thing I ever did was to give birth to my son. During labor, a baby's head usually lengthens to help it pass through the birth canal. Not my boy's. He was a gentle giant with a whopping head! It seems funny now, but when I was in labor, I worried that I would never get him out. My girls slipped through in a matter of moments. Not my son. In the midst of pain and pressure, I cried out, *"I can do all things through Christ who strengthens me"!* And Benjamin was born.

Build Yourself Up

"To gird" yourself, as in our key verse, means to wrap something around you. We gird ourselves with God's strength by wrapping His Word around our hearts and minds. We remind ourselves of His promises and speak them over our lives. That is the first step to real strength.

King David is an example to us all in this regard. As we discussed on Day 2, he and his army came home from battle one day to find their city destroyed. The place had been plundered, and the women and children had been taken captive. Reacting to the devastation, even David's most loyal followers pointed the finger at him and blamed him for their loss. David was distraught. So, what did he do? He built himself up in the Lord.

David was greatly distressed, for the men spoke of stoning him because the souls of them all were bitterly grieved, each man for his sons and daughters. But David encouraged and strengthened himself in the Lord his God. (1 Samuel 30:6 AMP)

How do we encourage ourselves? The same way we encourage others. We speak words of hope and faith.

We must choose to reject discouragement and doubt. We must refuse to think that we can't make it, and instead talk to ourselves like we would to a friend in need. Occasionally, when I am really struggling, I imagine that someone who has the same issues I am facing has come to see me for advice. I ask myself, *What would I say?* Then I do my best to follow the wisdom God would give me for that person! We need to learn to talk to ourselves with God's truth. As David often did, we can strengthen ourselves by declaring His Word.

Deborah was a leader who spoke to herself in order to build up her strength in the heat of battle, saying, "*O my soul, march on in strength!*" (Judges 5:21). The soul refers to our mind, our will, and our emotions. Put simply, it is what we think, want, and feel. Deborah was telling her thoughts and feelings to be strong. She was telling herself to be like a seasoned soldier: immune to ups and downs and focused on fulfilling the mission. The first time you speak to yourself in this way, it might feel strange. However, with practice, it will become your norm. Tell your heart what to think and then speak out words of encouragement. Sometimes, when our cars or our computers won't work, we talk to them, encouraging them to function the way they were meant to. (Some of us may even kick them!) Let's start speaking to our souls when they are weak or weary.

Be Consistent

As I shared earlier, our first child died before she was two years old. Naomi was not just our daughter—she was the church's baby, too. After she passed away, a friend ministered to our grieving congregation. I will never forget the heart of his message: "Continue doing what you know how to do." I believe that is the second secret to strength: carrying on through thick and thin. It is being consistent, whether you are happy or hurting. It is praising God on the mountaintop and in the valley alike. In truth, just by continuing, you can show strength when you are feeling weak.

> *She girds herself with strength [spiritual, mental, and physical fitness for her God-given task] and makes her arms strong and firm.*
>
> (Proverbs 31:17 AMP)

This verse in *The Amplified Bible* explains what strength is: *"spiritual, mental, and physical fitness."* When we are fit, we can carry on when others give up. We are ready for anything. And how do we get there? By training. The kind of training your soul needs is discipline. To be disciplined means to always do the right thing—whether you feel like it or not. Being consistent amid the normal ups and downs of life will build your stamina.

Strength is not a feeling. When a bodybuilder is at home relaxing, he does not *feel* powerful. Yet his capacity is proved when he lifts hefty weights. In the same way, we demonstrate our resilience by continuing to obey God even when we are in pain or under pressure. Difficult times are our opportunity to train and to grow. The book of James even tells us to be happy when we face tests and trials because, if we learn to endure, we will come out on the other side stronger.

> *If you faint in the day of adversity, your strength is small.*
>
> (Proverbs 24:10)

Be Strong

Remember that, four separate times, God told Joshua to *be* strong. (See Deuteronomy 31:23; Joshua 1:6, 7, 9.) Being strong is something we do, no matter how we feel. God did not tell Joshua to pray that He would make him mighty. Rather, He told him, "Be strong!" Your emotions will catch up with you if you step out. Practice *being* strong when you are tempted to give in. Practice makes perfect.

When I was in labor with my second child, I decided I wanted to stay as active as possible for as long as I could. I didn't want to rush to the hospital and sit around, so my husband and I went to a busy shopping mall to keep my mind off things. Every time a contraction came, I paused, breathed deeply, and continued on. As the labor pains got stronger, my reactions became more exaggerated. We stepped onto an escalator just as a massive contraction hit me. I hadn't realized that a small child was looking straight at me from the top of the stairs. The little guy screamed in fright as he saw me puffing like an injured dragon and hurtling toward him! The moral of the story? Strength is good, but we don't always look dignified while we're exercising it!

In Isaiah 27:5, God invites people to *"take hold of"* His strength; in Isaiah 52:1, we are instructed to *"put on"* our strength. In Proverbs 31:17, "girding oneself" with strength is commended. And, in Joshua 10:25, we are reminded to *"be strong."* Can you see the pattern? Strength is a choice— it corresponds to what we decide to think, say, and do.

TO DO TODAY

Which situation in your life is challenging you the most right now? Find a verse or passage in the Bible that gives God's perspective on it and/or His answer for it. Write out the verse or passage and stick it somewhere prominent. Confess it over your life every time you see it. Talk yourself into being strong.

PRAYER

[If you are going through a tough time, use this prayer:]

Dear Lord,

I thank You that You have great plans for my life. You have plans to prosper me and not to harm me, to give me a hope and a future. [*Remind yourself of God's Word concerning your circumstances. If you do not know what the Bible says about your situation, search for a verse or a passage that corresponds to it. If you are new to this practice, ask a friend or a leader to help you.*] My life is in Your hands! I choose today to continue doing what is right and good. I will study the Word even when I do not feel like it, and I will pray even when I feel low. I will continue to do the right thing. I take hold of Your strength. In Jesus' name, amen.

[If all is well, use this prayer:]

Dear Lord,

I am ready to be strong. The next time I go through trying circumstances, I will take captive every negative thought to the obedience of Christ and speak words of hope and faith to myself. I will continue doing what is right and good. I will take hold of Your strength. I will put it on and just "do it"! I give You praise that I am growing in Christ. In Jesus' name, amen.

TODAY'S TWEET:

I do the right thing, whether I'm happy or hurting. #detoxforyoursoul

DAY 27

Diligence

"Diligence is man's precious possession."
—Proverbs 12:27

One of our leaders discovered a blocked lavatory at our church building. He knew he could report it to the janitorial team and make it another person's problem, but he recognized that someone would have to sort out the mess. Gulping, rolling up a sleeve, and holding his nose, he plunged his bare hand into the dirty water (he hadn't been able to find any rubber gloves to use) and removed the offending debris from the toilet bowl. It wasn't a pretty sight or smell.

In our "instant" society, where comfort is king, we do not always appreciate the value of hard work. We might exert ourselves in pursuing our dreams. However, generally, we would rather relax than go the extra mile. By contrast, the Bible says that we should be conscientious in *all* that we do:

> *Whatever may be your task, work at it heartily (from the soul), as [something done] for the Lord and not for men.*
>
> (Colossians 3:23 AMP)

In the above verse, *"whatever"* means whatever—whether it excites me or not. As we discussed, the soul is made up of the mind, the will, and the emotions. So, Scripture is asking me to put both thought and feeling into everything I do. The example of Joseph inspires me. He was as industrious when he was working for no wages as he was when he was fulfilling his role as prime minister. He did not allow false accusations or imprisonment to stop him from serving steadfastly. Everywhere he went, he gave his best and proved himself dependable. Despite having been betrayed and abused, he gave 100 percent. I believe that is one of the attributes that set him apart from others and singled him out for promotion.

Diligence Must Be Applied

Our destiny is to fulfill our potential. That said, *achieving* our potential is not a foregone conclusion. To make our destiny definite, we have to apply ourselves with diligence.

Joshua was as faithful in assisting Moses as he subsequently was in commanding a nation. When his master told him to wait halfway up a mountain for forty days, he obeyed. I am sure that he prayed and praised while he waited, doing to the very best of his ability what he had been asked to do. There is not a single Bible hero who did not have to work hard—in good times and in bad.

In his letter to the church in Rome, Paul listed some of his expectations of Christians:

Not lagging in diligence, fervent in spirit, serving the Lord.
(Romans 12:11)

The Amplified Bible renders the above verse in this way: "*Never lag in zeal and in earnest endeavor....*" If you are normally industrious, check to see that you have not slackened. We can too easily begin to descend a slippery slope. Take time to think about the quality of your life and about your diligence at home, church, and work. Are you always willing to carry out tasks, and quick to do them? If you have never been very conscientious, it is time for a change.

But as you excel in everything—in faith, in speech, in knowledge, in all earnestness.... (2 Corinthians 8:7 ESV)

When we excel, we are leading the way, and we are at the top of the class. In the above verse, the apostle Paul congratulated the Corinthian believers for their exemplary attitudes and behavior. We need to emulate the positive traits of the early church and to grow more earnest every day.

> *Giving all diligence, add to your faith virtue, to virtue knowledge....*
> *For if these things are yours and abound, you will be neither barren nor*
> *unfruitful....* (2 Peter 1:5, 8)

We often talk about growing in faith or in wisdom, but we need to increase in conscientiousness, too. The Bible says that diligence is one of the keys to success. Perhaps you are dedicated to your job, but you grow weary in serving God. Maybe you are zealous when a task excites you but half-hearted when it is boring. Let us look within ourselves and evaluate our commitment. This is important. Diligence qualifies people for promotion:

> *The hand of the diligent will rule.* (Proverbs 12:24)

If we give our best when we are inspired *and* when we are not, we will excel. Have a guess at which important attribute the Bible says a leader must demonstrate. It is not power or charisma. It is diligence:

> *Having then gifts differing according to the grace that is given to us, let*
> *us use them:...he who leads, with diligence.* (Romans 12:6, 8)

Get the Job Done

We must make every effort to finish what we start. We all enjoy embarking on a new initiative—the excitement propels us. It is when the passion fades that we find out how committed we really are. Become someone who finishes well and gets the job done. Simply by completing tasks, you can set yourself apart as a reliable and dependable employee or leader. We must be conscientious and persistent. We should do everything with heartfelt commitment and to the best of our ability, demonstrating devotion even when it is difficult. Not only will the world notice, but God will see you and reward you.

Our key verse says,

> *Diligence is man's precious possession.*

Precious means "valuable," or "prized," while a possession is something we own. God wants us to hunt down and lay hold of diligence. It is a choice. For diligence to become a lifestyle for us, we must make a series of daily decisions to give our best, no matter what the task. When I sought God for greater excellence in my life, I mislaid three items within a week. I spent far too long looking for them and eventually asked the Holy Spirit for His help. First, He showed me where I had put them. Second, He explained what my problem was. I did not put things back where they belonged. I apologized to the Lord and embarked on a new habit. I would no longer allow myself to tidy things away in the wrong place, even if it meant I had to run upstairs several times in the space of five minutes! Diligence does not usually demand major change. It requires small adjustments, irrespective of the cost or inconvenience.

> *Whatever your hand finds to do, do it with all your might, for in the realm of the dead, where you are going, there is neither working nor planning nor knowledge nor wisdom.*   (Ecclesiastes 9:10 NIV)

Now is the time to prove your passion and your perseverance. The Lord will surely reward you.

TO DO TODAY

Evaluate the level of your diligence, taking into consideration your activities and endeavors at home, church, and work. What are you doing well? Where do you need to improve? Think about one change that would improve your performance in your everyday life. Commit to establishing that change by practicing it daily, starting today.

PRAYER

Father God,

You are so good. You always want the best for me. I thank You for the examples of Joseph, Joshua, Elisha, Deborah, and Paul, who all served steadfastly. I am sorry for the times when I have been slow or unwilling to do something I needed to do. I ask You to forgive me. I make a decision to be diligent and to give my best in all that I do. I commit to serving in Your house with devotion and commitment. Whatever You ask of me, I will do with all my heart and all my might. In Jesus' name, amen.

TODAY'S TWEET:

God deserves my best. #detoxforyoursoul

DAY 28

The Right Friends

"Walk with the wise and become wise;
associate with fools and get in trouble."
—Proverbs 13:20 (NLT)

When I went to university, my mum prayed that God would give me two good Christian friends. Within days of my arrival, her prayer was answered when I met Pip and Clare. It was not long before the three of us were great buddies. Although I loved the Lord, as the months went by and the temptations multiplied, my heart grew cold toward the things of God. Soon, I was living a double life. Although I attended church, I went to the wrong places with the wrong people (and, not surprisingly, got hurt along the way). Nonetheless, my friends stood by me. Clare would pray for me night after night, while Pip reassured me of her unchanging friendship. I believe they are two of the reasons why I am who I am today. When I rededicated my life to the Lord, their prayer lists instantly halved!

Every Relationship Should Be Fruitful

The righteous should choose his friends carefully, for the way of the wicked leads them astray. (Proverbs 12:26)

The way of the wicked leads the righteous—not the wicked—astray. God longs for you to hit the mark, but Satan wants you to flounder and to fail. Your close friends will either help you or hinder you. They will either build you up or pull you down. So, you should be careful about whom you hang around with. I believe that *every* relationship in our lives should be fruitful—either you support the other person, the other person helps you, or you encourage each other.

Today's verse explains that we become like our friends. We will probably end up going where they go, doing what they do, and saying what they say. If you want to grow in God, you need to consider whom you call your companions. Do they help you to stay on the straight and narrow? Do they encourage you on to greater things? Or do they lead you astray, cause you to compromise, or even knock your faith?

A dear friend who has a mighty ministry in Ghana always prays with his left hand over his ear. I think it is his way of reminding himself that communication with God must be a two-way street. We listen while God talks, and God graciously listens while we talk. When this minister in Ghana is in strong prayer, he invariably has his hand against his ear and his eyes tightly shut. He is a spiritual father who has raised up many sons and daughters in the faith in that nation. I was tickled pink when I visited his church and saw people all over the place using exactly the same motions when they prayed! He never taught them to pray that way. They just picked up his habit from being around him.

Again, it is human nature to become like the people we spend the most time with. On one occasion, our worship leader was praying aloud, and I did a double take—it was like listening to myself! She was interceding with a similar strength and authority. Whether you like it or not, you will be influenced by your friends.

Spend Time with People Who Build You Up

My friends scorn me; my eyes pour out tears to God.   (Job 16:20)

Job might well have been better off without his so-called friends. Rather than comforting him, they criticized him. They kicked him when he was down. If my companions do not build my faith when I am faltering, they are probably no more helpful than Job's buddies. We need to surround ourselves with people who will strengthen us when times are tough. We should spend time with those who encourage us on to greater things.

Jesus said,

You are My friends if you do whatever I command you. (John 15:14)

The Lord defines a true friend as someone who does God's will. So, if you want to grow, you must be with people who will truly build you up— those who will inspire you and challenge you, those who will help you to keep on the right track. We get only one chance at living our lives, so we need all the help we can get to do it right.

As iron sharpens iron, so a man sharpens the countenance of his friend. (Proverbs 27:17)

God wants to place friends in your life who will help you to achieve your God-given potential. Sometimes, we need to clear out the old so that we can bring in the new. If you are surrounded by people who drag you down, it might be time to ask God for His help to make some changes. Maybe you should distance yourself from those who hinder you. Doing so can be painful, but it will be worth it in the long run. Sometimes, we go through seasons of separation. It is not easy, but it may be just a temporary measure. If you really want to become your best (and I believe you do), this is an important step in the right direction.

At the same time, I encourage you to treasure those who help you to be your best. Thank God for their lives and treat them with love and respect. Invest in such friendships. Make time for those who build your faith and encourage you toward true success.

TO DO TODAY

Take a few moments to evaluate your friendships. Make a list of the people with whom you spend most of your spare time. Who strengthens you? Who pulls you down? Which relationships are fruitful, and which are damaging? Resolve to distance yourself from anyone who discourages you. Decide how you will go about this. Then make an appointment this week to meet up with someone who will inspire you.

PRAYER

Father God,

Thank You for Your love for me. I realize that I am affected by the people around me. So, I lay down my friendships before You today. I pray that You will show me who helps me and who hinders me. I ask You to place people in my life who will challenge me and encourage me. I will protect those relationships and value those friendships. I want Your best, so I ask for Your help to separate myself from friends who bring me down or lead me astray. I am so grateful for companions who build me up. Thank You, Lord. In Jesus' name, amen.

TODAY'S TWEET:

True friends will help me to become my best. #detoxforyoursoul

DAY 29

Boldness

"The righteous are bold as a lion."
—Proverbs 28:1

After I rededicated my life to the Lord, I went out on the streets of London to share the gospel every Saturday. When I felt good, I went. When I felt afraid, I went. That is how I learned to be bold.

Have I not commanded you? Be strong and courageous. Do not be afraid; do not be discouraged, for the LORD your God will be with you wherever you go. (Joshua 1:9 NIV)

God did not encourage Joshua to be courageous. He *commanded* him to be so. In fact, as we've previously noted, on four separate occasions, the Lord told him that he *must* be bold. It is always God who does the miracles, but He works through people. Israel's destiny depended upon Joshua being brave. Likewise, every remarkable endeavor demands courage. This is the case whether, for example, you want to start a new business or go for a significant promotion. It is the same if you long to share the gospel with friends or launch a new ministry. You need great confidence.

Take Authority over Fear and Discouragement

But how do we become courageous? When my son was about six years old, he asked me the same question: "Mummy, how do you become bold?" I went through the Scriptures with him, line upon line. After about five minutes, he turned to me with a quizzical look on his face and said, "But Mummy, can't you just go to the hairdresser and get it all cut off?" He had gotten the words *bold* and *bald* totally confused! Unfortunately, the barber can't really help us with boldness. Thankfully, the Bible can. When the Word exhorts us to be brave, it usually instructs us to deal with two problems first: fear and discouragement. (See, for example, Joshua 1:9, above.)

Fear is a spirit. Yet the Bible says, *"Resist the devil and he will flee from you. Draw near to God and He will draw near to you"* (James 4:7–8). We need to take authority over the spirit of fear through prayer. Fear is an enemy of God, just as much as sin and sickness are. We must not tolerate it in any area of our lives. It always seeks to hinder and to harm. Let us become determined to eradicate all intimidation from our hearts and minds. Fear suffocates and stifles, but the Holy Spirit brings liberty.

Then we need to deal with discouragement. Again, we make a choice in this matter. We remind ourselves of God's promises and refuse to be forlorn. If we dwell on difficulties, we will feel downhearted. However, if we think about God's goodness, our spirits will be lifted. To do this, we need to build our faith. When we focus on His power rather than on our inadequacy, our confidence will grow. When we remind ourselves not only that He is able but also that *we are able through Him*, our faith will be strengthened, and we will be equipped to address our discouragement.

You Will Find Your Boldness!

When Asa heard these words and the prophecy…he took courage….
(2 Chronicles 15:8)

To become bold, we have to *do* something. King Asa heard the Word and took courage. I love the way *The Message* version puts this verse: *"Asa heard the prophecy…, took a deep breath, then rolled up his sleeves, and went to work."* That is how we *take* courage.

Likewise, Ezra, the priest and scribe, reminded himself that God was with him when he led a group of Israelites back to Jerusalem after the captivity. He drew confidence from that knowledge, and he chose to be bold:

Because the hand of the LORD *my God was on me, I took courage....*
(Ezra 7:28 NIV)

It is all too easy for us to believe that we are weak or timid. Perhaps you think you could never speak in public, start a business, or share the gospel with a stranger. However, if you will dig deep within yourself, you will discover great daring. You are made in the image of God, and He is always strong. Usually, you can find something only when you are looking for it. If you are determined enough, you will find the boldness you need. David found boldness based on God's faithfulness and love toward him:

[David said,] *Your servant has found courage....*
(2 Samuel 7:27 NIV)

One of the ways in which the devil tries to control Christians is by making us afraid to open our mouths. However, anything God says, we can repeat with confidence. Anywhere God sends us, we can boldly travel to.

[God] *Himself has said, "I will never leave you nor forsake you." So we may boldly say: "The* LORD *is my helper; I will not fear. What can man do to me?"*
(Hebrews 13:5–6)

When God says something, that settles the matter. He has promised that He will not leave us or let us down. That is all we need. We can speak with incredible boldness, knowing that the Lord is our Guide, our Helper, and our Protector. Put simply, having courage is not a feeling—it is a choice. It is a command from God that we decide to obey. Let us take courage and speak with boldness. Then let us move forward and *be* bold!

Act with courage, and may the LORD *be with those who do well.*
(2 Chronicles 19:11 NIV)

TO DO TODAY

Ask yourself, "What or who makes me afraid?" Then think about your family, your ministry, your work, and your recreation. Is there anything that you desire to do but have lacked the courage to try? Maybe you once stepped out to try something but got knocked down. You need to get back up. You do not have to tolerate feeling intimidated anymore. In the name of Jesus, bind the spirit of fear and command it to stop tormenting you. Then decide what you will do to take courage. That might mean completing the first paragraph of the book you want to write. Maybe you need to call a specific friend or visit a particular relative. Perhaps you have always wanted to join the choir but have never had the confidence to put your name forward. Do something brave today toward fulfilling God's purposes for your life. Then decide what you will do tomorrow.

PRAYER

Father God,

Thank You for freedom! You have not given me a spirit of timidity but of power, love, and a sound mind. I take authority over all fear in my life. I renounce all feelings of intimidation and cowardice. I am sorry for giving in to fear and allowing it to control me. Today, I rise up against the spirit of fear and rebuke it in Jesus' mighty name! I am a child of God, and that makes me a conqueror.

Where I have easily become downhearted, I change my ways. I will remember Your love and kindness toward me. I thank You for everything You have done for me. [Now thank the Lord for four or five different blessings in your life.] I stir myself up today. I take courage and choose to be brave. I take confidence and use the power You have given me. I can do all things through Christ who strengthens me. I will obey Your commandment to be courageous. I declare that I am bold, and I give You praise! In the name of Jesus, amen.

TODAY'S TWEET:

I will do something brave today. #detoxforyoursoul

DAY 30

Filled Anew

"Surely I will pour out my spirit on you."
—Proverbs 1:23

Some people have difficulty delegating responsibility. I don't. I love having help! However, certain people avoid asking others for assistance because of previous bad experiences in this regard. My husband knew a family of eight in Ireland. The mother was desperate for a break, so she asked her children to clean the house while she was away. Eight smiling faces met her as she returned, delighted with their efforts to improve their home. Not only had they cleaned the place, but they had painted it, too. The problem was, they had painted not only the doors but also the windows and floors. Needless to say, she never accepted their offer of assistance again!

The Holy Spirit, Our Friend

It is amazing how much support the Holy Spirit offers us if we ask Him—and His help is by no means amateur. The Bible describes the Spirit as our aid. Some schools assign older (and wiser) students to support younger pupils and to show them the ropes. The Holy Spirit has been appointed by the Father to help you and me as we serve God.

But the Helper, the Holy Spirit, whom the Father will send in My name, He will teach you all things. (John 14:26)

I love the way *The Message* Bible puts this verse: *"The Friend, the Holy Spirit...will make everything plain to you."* The Holy Spirit is your companion. He comes alongside you to help. Whether you are struggling or soaring, He is your best support.

I have a friend who has stuck by me through thick and thin. We walk, talk, laugh, cry, and relax together. There is nothing that I cannot share with her. That is the kind of relationship the Holy Spirit seeks to have with you. The above verse in *The Amplified Bible* shows the extent of the Spirit's assistance:

> But the Comforter (Counselor, Helper, Intercessor, Advocate, Strengthener, Standby), the Holy Spirit, Whom the Father will send in My name [in My place, to represent Me and act on My behalf], He will teach you all things.

When you need support, He is the One who can give it. When you need to talk, He is there to listen. When you need strength, He will provide it. There is nothing too small or too big for Him.

Blessings and Benefits from the Spirit

Too often, we think we need to help God, but He wants to assist us. In truth, we cannot fulfill our purpose without Him. He is our Comforter, Encourager, and Confidant. There are a whole host of other blessings and benefits that He brings. The following are some of them.

Refreshing: If you have been feeling weak or weary, there is nothing like the revitalizing presence of God. The Bible says, *"Repent therefore and be converted,....so that times of refreshing may come from the presence of the Lord"* (Acts 3:19). In fact, it is good to be refreshed even when you are strong. Jesus showed us what we should do when He said to His disciples, *"**Receive** the Holy Spirit"* (John 20:22). We need to go to God in prayer, ask for a fresh touch of His Spirit, and then *receive*. Accept the Holy Spirit in the same way you receive a gift. Put your arms out, ready for your infilling. If you have never done this before, I encourage you to study Acts 2:1–4 and Acts 19:1–6. Ask God to baptize you with His precious Spirit. If you have done this a thousand times, do it again so that He can replenish you in His presence.

Power: If you want to live life to the full, you need power.

The Holy Spirit will come upon you, and the power of the Highest will overshadow you. (Luke 1:35)

The Holy Spirit gives us the power to witness, the power to heal, the power to preach, the power to prosper, and the power to live in victory. The great news is that the Spirit comes with it all! Miraculous might is available. We just need to ask in faith and believe that we receive.

Boldness: Even boldness can be received supernaturally. The Bible tells us that the apostles were intimidated by the threats of religious leaders. They prayed, and God showed up in great power and released new boldness:

And when they had prayed, the place where they were assembled together was shaken; and they were all filled with the Holy Spirit, and they spoke the word of God with boldness. (Acts 4:31)

Freedom: We were not designed to live in bondage. The Lord wants us to be at liberty to do and to say what is right and good. He longs for us to feel free in His presence. I have watched people shout and dance before the Lord as they break free from years of self-consciousness. That is what the Spirit does! I have seen folk who used to be constrained by the fear of man find freedom. That is the will of God.

Where the Spirit of the Lord is, there is liberty. (2 Corinthians 3:17)

I started today's message by saying that the Holy Spirit is your Friend. He is always looking to draw nearer to you. He longs for greater companionship with you, and He wants to release more of His power and His presence in your life. He wants you to be on fire for God, burning with love.

The fire never says, "Enough!" (Proverbs 30:16)

Never become satisfied with your knowledge of the Lord. Never become content with the anointing on your life. Always ask for more. God is ready to give. He wants to fill you afresh with His wonderful Spirit. Enjoy!

TO DO TODAY

Think about what is going on in your life at the moment. You may have a specific need that you know God can meet. Perhaps the need is for boldness or for freedom. As you finish your detox, I'm sure you would like to receive new power to fulfill your God-given purpose. Quiet your heart and ask God to do something new within you today. He will seal the work He has done in your life this month with a fresh touch of His wonderful Spirit.

PRAYER

Father God,

You are all I need. I thank You that You are always willing and able to fill me afresh. I am hungry for more of You. I am thirsty for more of Your Spirit. I need more of Your presence. I need more power, more boldness, more freedom, more love, and more anointing. I ask You to come and fill me by Your Spirit. Open the floodgates of heaven and let Your sweet Spirit rain down on me. [*Now remain in prayer with your arms outstretched. Sing a song of worship and wait for His fresh touch. He is faithful.*] I am so grateful for Your wonderful presence and awesome power. Thank You for everything You have done in me during the past month. As Psalm 119:50 [AMP] says, "*Your word has revived me*"!

I give You all the praise and glory. In Jesus' name, amen.

TODAY'S TWEET:

I've completed the 30-day detox for my soul.
#detoxforyoursoul

What Next?

This is just the beginning. Build on everything God has done in your life. If the Holy Spirit took you through a major overhaul, continue in your newfound strength. If there are certain areas in which you want more help, go back to the corresponding messages in this book and continue to apply the principles found there. Study the Word of God and find other relevant books that can assist you. You can redo the detox as often as you like. Most important, do not stay in the same place spiritually. Keep moving. Always press onward and upward.

> *I am convinced and sure of this very thing, that He Who began a good work in you will continue until the day of Jesus Christ [right up to the time of His return], developing [that good work] and perfecting and bringing it to full completion in you.* (Philippians 1:6 AMP)

Let the above words sink deep into you. God is preparing you for your destiny. He has already started the job, and He will be faithful to finish it. Take some time to thank God for His goodness.

I would love to hear your testimony of what God did in your life as you detoxed. If you would like to share, please visit www.jonaughton.com, click on "Share a testimony," and then send me your story. God has an awesome purpose for your life. Stay close to Jesus and see what He will do.

An Invitation

If you would like to ask Jesus into your heart to become the Lord of your life, I would be honored to lead you in a simple prayer. The Bible says that God loves you and that Jesus wants to draw close to you.

> Behold, I stand at the door and knock. If anyone hears My voice and opens the door, I will come in.... (Revelation 3:20)

To know Jesus as your Friend, your Savior, and your Lord, the first step is to ask. Pray this prayer:

Dear Lord,

I know that You love me and have a wonderful plan for my life. I ask You to come into my heart today and be my Savior and Lord. Thank You that, because You died on the cross for me, I am forgiven of every wrong I have ever committed, and I am completely cleansed from my past. I give my life to You entirely and ask You to lead me in Your ways from now on. In Jesus' name, amen.

If you have prayed this prayer for the first time, I would love to hear from you via my Web site, jonaughton.com. Also, it is important to tell a Christian friend what you prayed, and to find a good church. Just as a newborn baby needs nourishment and care, so you (and all Christians) need the support of other believers as you start your new life as a follower of Jesus Christ.

At www.harvestchurch.org.uk, you can listen free to Bible messages that will help to build your faith. You can follow me on Twitter (@naughtonjo), go on Facebook and like my public page (Jo Naughton), and/or become a Facebook friend of Harvest Church London.

God bless you!

About the Author

Together with her husband, Paul, Jo Naughton pastors Harvest Church in London, England. A public relations executive turned pastor, Jo's previous career included working for Prince Charles as an executive VP of his largest charity. After reaching the pinnacle of the public relations world, Jo felt the call of God to full-time ministry. She is a regular monthly guest on the UK's leading Christian radio station, where she is affectionately known as the "Soul Doctor," and she is a regular contributor to Christian magazines. An international speaker and author, Jo ministers with great personal honesty in conferences, conventions, and churches across America, Europe, Africa, and Asia with a heart-piercing anointing. Thousands of people have testified to having received powerful and life-changing healings, both emotional and spiritual. Jo and Paul have two wonderful children, Benjamin and Abigail.

You can connect with Jo via:

www.jonaughton.com
Facebook (public page—Jo Naughton)
Twitter (@naughtonjo)

For more information about Harvest Church London,
visit www.harvestchurch.org.uk.

Welcome to Our House!

We Have a Special Gift for You

It is our privilege and pleasure to share in your love of Christian books. We are committed to bringing you authors and books that feed, challenge, and enrich your faith.

To show our appreciation, we invite you to sign up to receive a specially selected **Reader Appreciation Gift**, with our compliments. Just go to the Web address at the bottom of this page.

God bless you as you seek a deeper walk with Him!

WE HAVE A GIFT FOR YOU. VISIT:

whpub.me/nonfictionthx

WHITAKER
HOUSE